WHY I NEVER GAVE UP

AN INSPIRATION ON THE PATH TO OVERCOMING ADVERSITY

BY

PRINCESS .N. SIZIBA

TABLE OF CONTENT

DEDICATION

I dedicate this book to my daughter Unathi Rachel Mpofu and my brother Terence Siziba. I love you both so much and l pray this book serves as a reminder that you are a gift to this world. Claim it, believe it and walk in it.

I also dedicate it to every person who ever thought of giving up at any point in their lives; because they believed they had nothing positively substantial to live for. Within you lies gifts and abilities yet to be discovered, you too have something incredible to serve to this world.

ACKNOWLEDGEMENT

All this would not have been possible without God, to Him I owe everything.

Would also like to thank my family in California; uncle Charles, aunty Siphi, Mzie, Samu and Sam for the sacrifices they made for this book to be published, I'm ever so grateful. To all my friends who fueled my gift and believed in me, thank you for the encouragement and reassurance, it made me want to do even better.

To my parents; thank you for being patient with me.

To Pastor Ben Achero thank you for giving me the opportunity to proof read one of your books, it planted seeds of greatness in me. To Pastor Judy Achero, thank you for being the voice of reason in my life. l call to mind the day you said to me, "you need to start writing books." l was in so much despair and self-doubt because l had just lost a huge part of the manuscript of what l thought would be my first book. You assured me that the new content will come, and it surely did.

Joy Eunice and Rue Mada, your great efforts are truly appreciated.

Thank you.

Thank you to everyone who made a positive impact in my journey.

INTRODUCTION

The world is full of broken people; heart shattered lives dressed in Armani suits and red bottom shoes. On the outside it looks so appealing and picture perfect, but one could never reckon that beneath lies a deeply wounded man or woman battling depression, hopeless thoughts, rage, bitterness and concealing a bleeding heart. We live in a world where broken can be dressed up so beautifully. Flawlessly arched brows, good hair and a slap of red lipstick for that superficial confidence, but on the inside is an empty space. A soul silently screaming for help; "a black hole in obscurity."

How do l know this, one may ask? I know this because I once was that broken person, and for as long as l can remember, pain was all l knew and identified with. My own experiences opened my eyes to the consciousness that there were so many people out in the world, who resembled who l was. As l dug deeper, l got a great intuitive grasp of reality that people deal with these manners of issues on a daily basis with no one possibly ever knowing it. They put so much effort in hiding their flaws out of fear of judgement that they don't have it together. So, they bottle it in, until they are consumed by it. By day they are masters of disguise, but by night they are drenched in an ocean of tears, finally revealing who they are behind the mask.

How many times have we heard of a tragedy and in complete disbelief point out how happy of a person we thought he or she was on the outside, yet in essence they were slowly fading away on the inside? They trended on social media, their feel-good statuses were the highlight of the day, how could they have not been okay? It doesn't matter how influential or popular you are, or whatever walk of life you may come from. The reality is, there are certain things that can bring you to your knees. It could be heartbreak, debt, divorce, betrayal, rejection, poverty or anything undesirable, and the way you choose to deal with it, will determine whether you succumb to your circumstances, or instead overcome them. My "aha" moment came when I had an epiphany of that, it all narrows down to the mind and the thoughts you allow to have power and influence in the face of adversity. It is how you begin to control and strengthen your mental and emotional process that determines if you will prevail over your circumstance. Your mental resilience is what will condition your win or defeat.

There are people across the world contemplating on taking their lives because their partner left them for someone else, some are drowning in debt and just can't seem to find a way out of the ruins. Others have children they are struggling to provide for, and for some; it's failing businesses. A portion are homeless and don't know where their next meal will come from. For several it's the pressure of not having a career at a certain age at which society says; they should have excelled and settled by then. It could also be an individual who has just lost a loved one and don't know how to deal with the grief. Somebody somewhere has been left at harm's way and is clueless as to how they can pick up the fragmented pieces. When there's insurmountable pressure, the easy way out always seems to be ending everything.

It is because in those moments people cannot imagine anything better to live for. Imagination is a mind thing more than it is a heart thing. When your mind caves in, it cripples your will to go on and giving up soon trails as a result of that. If the enemy can just have your mind, he knows he has firm grip on you; so you've got to fight for your mind and recondition it. When your mindset has been revitalized you begin to approach life differently. Composure becomes your strength, you begin to face situations with courage and pray with reassurance, you become less anxious and more at peace. That is the winning mentality everybody should possess.

Time and again we need a little motivation to keep mentally strong and that adversity doesn't seal our fate. You have to learn how to look at every situation with the eyes of hope and revelation that, there is a way out, and it begins with changing your thought pattern. Even after everything you may have experienced, the fact that you're still here is God's way of saying, live! "I see you're wounded but live. I see you're broken but live. I saw what they did to you but live. I know you just lost everything but live. I saw the weighty mistake but live. I saw the way you were mishandled but live. I see the debt stacked against you, the struggles and turmoil but I want you to live because; I am the way out of anything and everything."

In my book I share the things that strengthened me and proved helpful in my own journey, I also confer the godly perspective on the challenges we face as we go through life. I share the reasons why I never gave up and it all began with changing the way I think. That soon created the wave effect of aligning with my purpose, developing courage, walking by faith and so many positives that led me to where I am today. Your journey to healing and not giving up is a combination of so many elements but foremost, "you must get your mind right." Rise above the issue in your mind first, challenge yourself to begin to think on and believe better. One of the things that God started working on in me, was my mind. There can be a disharmony in your thoughts, heart and prayers. You can pray but at the same time have your mind swamped with thoughts of how everything is so wide of the mark in your life, and can never get better. Once I worked on my mind and reconditioned it to right thinking, I noticed how so many things began to shift in a positive direction.

When I was thoughtfully considering what the title of this book would be, I came across a heart wrenching post on social media. A young lady in distress was intending on taking her own life because things were so burdensome for her. Seeing that really tugged at my heart, how many more others out there were just like her? In an attempt to somehow contribute positively l thought of starting a thread on social media with the hashtag, "why l never gave up." In that moment l knew that would be a remarkable title for the book as it would resonate with many and show them that there is hope, no matter the circumstances they may be faced with. People are looking for answers, they are seeking that one or many other reasons to face another day. Many are in search of solutions that will not only speak to the depths of their being, but will sustain them for a lifetime. It is my desire that if l share what motivated me to keep strong, you will find a reason to hold on too. As you read this book may you gather the strength to get up and go on.

You are reading this book because l never gave up.

DON'T GIVE UP!

————— ⟨⁓⁓⟩ —————

A Word Of Challenge From The Author

A word of challenge from the author

THE MINDSET

————— ⋅◆⋅ —————

I first want to converse about the mind because it is one of the underwriting factors of getting out of distress. Until your mind is out of the gutter, it becomes a challenge to break out of adversity.

The mind is a very powerful and dominant thing, one that can be renewed, ruled and directed in turn determining what course your life can take. Your mind is so influential that it can manifest your thoughts in the logic that, what you mentally see becoming a reality, can actually happen. It is true that the mind has an eye and if you can perceptually see yourself in a certain place, the probabilities are you will get there. It could be seeing yourself whole, in good health, great wealth, at peace, out of debt, educated or successful. Whatever it is, because your mind is so convinced of it and you firmly believe in that truth; it soon becomes a reality.

Think of your mind as the place of your blueprint. The place where you can design, map and model the life you want to see manifest.

How can one then apply that positive principle? The same way you go to the gym to strengthen your muscles, is the same way you can empower your mind by carefully and prudently choosing what you meditate or think on. In his book, *"As a man thinketh"* James Allen says, "a man can choose his thoughts." So, to a great extent, it all comes down to a choice, not a feeling. You have better control of your mind than you do your heart because; you don't necessarily have to feel something to choose the right thought. It is waking up each morning with strong resolve that you will think on better and greater things despite what may be happening around you. It is being intentional about your thoughts and daily regulating them by casting down the negative, and elevating the positive.

When you incessantly and consistently think on the right things, it is reinforced in your mind and heart so much that you can handle anything thrown on your path, with an optimistic attitude. It is not being in denial of the negative that may be going on around you, but rather acknowledging it but still choosing to focus your mental energy on a positive conclusion. Therefore, it is of great importance that what you say to yourself in thought, be things that build and not tear down. Depending on which thoughts you harbor and focus on, they can govern the path your life can take.

When you come into this world, you are in the primitive of your innocence and all is pure in your sight. You have not felt the sting of the unfavorable or seen things for what they candidly are. But as you grow older and your development broadens, you begin to understand and question the ample of life. You question why you had to be betrayed? Why did it have to be you who was adopted? Why did your marriage fail? Why did you have to experience failure and heartache? Why the disability? Why did you get rejected? Why did you have to come from a broken family?

The Mindset

Why is your career in the rut? Why can't you seem to keep a relationship and settle down? Why did your business fail?

These are true representations of the challenges that people try to confront, almost on a daily basis. The things we go through immensely affect the way we think. Whether it's sickness, loss of loved one, heartbreak, physical limitations, pain, anger, debt or fame; all these have a bearing on the way we perceive life. After having experienced so much, people often become worn out and choose to conform to their circumstances and do life defeated. There is a sense of being overwhelmed by their griefs because on the sidelines they are dealing with depression, suicidal thoughts, poverty, pain and worry. For this reason; as you go through life, there is a renewing of the mind that needs to charge in because of the damaging and unkind things you may have experienced or are going through. Things to be undone and repaired in your mind so much that you condition it to right thinking. In doing so, you become a strong and upright minded individual.

Romans 12: 2, placed it the best way plausible:

"And be not conformed to this world, but be ye transformed by the renewing of your mind." (KJV)

Transformation is the aftermath of a renewed mind. Your life can change for better if you can alter the way you think because, it is what will determine whether you yield to your afflictions or come out victorious.

As I've matured my eyes have been opened to the view point that, God is supreme and has the power to change anything, but we have the responsibility to have the conviction and a positive mindset. Your emotional state does not make God untrue, whether you feel it or not. All hell can be breaking loose in your life and everything may be evidently overwhelming, but if you can master the discipline of being calm in mind and not anxious, you have just uncovered the strength of balance and overcoming in every situation. Personally, I've had experiences that almost slew me but through the process; l discovered some positives. I had to learn truths about what God says regarding the negative: depression, worry, hurt, revenge, rage, bitterness and what He says about the positive: purpose, love, peace, and so many other things that affect our walk in this daily life. I learned the unbelievable power of practicing calmness of mind and self-control in the midst of the most chaotic circumstances. I also learned to keep my emotions in balance, and the value of composure even in the face of adversity.

Unpleasant experiences first consume and overwhelm your heart, don't let them get to your mind too; save one. When you train your mind and accustom yourself to right thinking, change is inevitable. To every negative there is a positive, you just need to look for it. I draw confidence from Romans 8:28 as it appropriates that:

> *"That is why we can be so sure that every detail in our lives of love for God, is worked into something good." (MSGE)*

If you can get up each morning and say, l will disregard whatever may be happening around me and instead, firmly believe that things will change for better; you have just taken hold of your power.

WHY I NEVER GAVE UP

PART 1

I CHANGED THE WAY I THINK

This book was birthed at a time when I was truly learning how to trust God through every circumstance, and someway learn to adopt the power of positive thinking and apply it in my daily life. Things were so tumultuous and my feelings were all over the place.

I was broken, hurting, tired, frustrated, weary, bitter, depressed, you name it; "I was just a mess." Nothing was working and everything was going in an unfavorable direction so much that it felt like torture to be alive. There was no telling my feelings to hush, I was mostly existing to ooze tears because all I did was cry, day and night that became the new normal for me. I was flooded with so many emotions but soon saw the light of that in the midst of all the disarray, the thing that I truly had better control of, was my mind.

Somewhere in the realm of my mind I knew I had to keep it together if I was going to survive this and make it out of valley. Despite everything that was emerging, there was an inner piece of me that still wanted to pull through and come out on the other side having overcome; but l just didn't know how. In the process of trying to figure it out I had to confront the situation and get to grips with what was happening in that moment. It wasn't good but l didn't want it to kill me; I didn't want to lose my mind.

I vividly remember sitting down and thinking, l won't make it out of this alive if l let these emotions consume me and allow my mind to cave in; l will just lose it! One afternoon in the midst of my then chaotic life, l had a conversation with myself. We've all had those moments where life gets frantic and you go back and forth in your mind trying to make sense of everything. I recognized the reality of the situation for what it was, but how could l turn all the adverse emotions l was feeling into something positive? What were the opposites of these awful feelings that were just ready to throw me over? I knew that whatever it came to, l couldn't be defeated in my mind and in that moment, one of the first things that l had the disclosure of was; "l had to deal with my mind." It was my biggest obstacle and l knew it could be such a drawback in my trying to heal, move forward and progress. There were things that needed to be undone and reformed in my mind.

So little by little l committed to the process of learning how to gain the upper hand over my emotions, subdue my thoughts and make them aid to my growth and strength. But let me tell you, "it was a jagged road." This was probably one of the most grueling things I ever had to do. On some days I didn't want to get out of bed, I wanted to be left alone and so desperately craved the misery to end but a part of me knew that giving up would have meant I have come to the end of me.

I had to drag myself out of bed and find comfort in that "this too shall pass." Some days I felt strong but others not so much. I would get swamped with feelings of hopelessness, emptiness, pain and irritability. I fought so hard to keep my judgements in check when those emotions were raging as I did not want to harbor anything that was impediment to my becoming a better person. When I felt negative thoughts arising, I would begin to write down the positive about myself or the situation. Yes, I wrote it down. I would also say out loud the opposite of what I was feeling, but it wasn't without struggle. Some days I would reason out that it was too hard and my mind is exhausted but would still push myself. I was training my mind to do something it wasn't accustomed to so I had to be patient with myself because it was going to take time. Change is not achieved short of effort. I was the kind that used to succumb to negative thinking, so, challenging my own thoughts was very intense.

You see, sometimes the fight of faith is in your mind. It's in moments when you subconsciously give power to your current situation. It's when you replay scenes of what went awry and then reliving the pain all over again. It's when you rationalize based on facts if things can ever get better for you. Often when something is wrong, we begin to worry and sweat it out in our minds. What am I going to do? Will things ever work out for me? Will my life ever get better? Will I ever have a career? Can I possibly be healed? Will I ever experience authentic love? There must be something wrong with me? Right there in those moments, those are the thoughts we should shut down instantly before they become seeds in our minds.

When negative thoughts intensify, they turn into worry, depression, anxiety, heaviness and soon weigh you down, not only mentally but physically too. In my situation it became clear-cut that, if I could change my thoughts to reassuring ones, my feelings and body will in turn be in harmony with my mind, and so will the world around me. In that season I learned how to countervail negative thoughts with beautiful ones. I don't know what your circumstance is, maybe its years of distress, maybe your career is nonexistent, it could be disappointment, heartbreak, failures or sickness, but you need to recognize that your mind can be renewed in turn transforming your life.

I had to speak greatness about myself in moments l thought l would never amount to anything. I had to say it out loud that, "I'm an amazing woman and l will change the world. l am worthy, l am a woman of real distinction, yes l am honorable, l am phenomenal and God is on my side." I had to say it out loud to reinforce things l did not believe about myself at the time, but it began to grow on me and l slowly started to truly believe it and that my life would change. There was hope for me after everything l had endured. Philippians 4 vs 8 says:

"Fix your thoughts on what is true, and honorable, and right, and pure, and lovely and admirable. Think on things that are excellent and worthy of praise." (NLT)

Getting out of that place of distress and defeat all starts in the mind. Be wary of careless thoughts, ones that are barren, fruitless and vain. Dare to stretch your mind to trust that things can get better, and that where you are is not a dead end.

Life has many hurdles and your experiences might have deeply hurt you and may have been unfair but the evidence of life in you, is sufficient motive to get up each morning knowing that there's better that awaits on the other side of adversity. These are some of the things l comforted myself with and as you read through some of the affirmations l share, personalize and speak them out loud, let it unleash the warrior in you and take you places you never thought conceivable. Let it be a daily reminder of who you are and the power you possess because as we go through life, we soon forget that our greatest power lies within. Sometimes all it requires of you is that you change your thoughts, so you can set in motion events that could completely permute your life. Years of negative thinking need to be slowly weaned off your mind. When a mother weans off her child she breastfeeds less and slowly begins to introduce more solids. The baby will cry because the adjustment is uncomfortable, but it is beneficial and pivotal to its growth. It goes the same way when you're training your mind to shift to right thinking. You will cry and throw temper tantrums, you will be so frustrated and irritable because the change is new and intolerable to you but in the long run you will grow. Growth does not come without introducing something new.

I never gave up because l changed the way l think. Are you observing your though process? Are you willing to change your thoughts?

I WON IN MY MIND FIRST

———— ·◆ 🦋 ◆· ————

In a world where mental well-being has become such a cause for concern, it is critical that people learn composure and gain psycho-logical strength to be able to handle life's challenges with positivity. It is often so easy to convince your mind that things will go wrong, than it is that they will get better. But as you grow and accustom your mind to right thinking, it becomes a little easier to be optimistic. Growth should not only be seen as a physical thing, but a mental one too. Many are focused on enhancing their muscles but neglecting their minds. If you can elevate your mind to get there first, the rest will follow. But first; "you have to win in your mind."

To show how powerful the mind is, there was a day l was exercising at home, nothing too tedious, just a few planks and squats. But because l hadn't done so in a while, my body began to feel so tired in such a short amount of time. Embarrassed at my own lack of tenacity, l became even more determined to push harder. I set a target in my mind and kept saying within myself "ok just a little longer, just a couple of more squats," and l pushed for another minute or so. I only stopped when my mind whispered, "ok l can't go further than this."

I know this experience was just an exercise and what others would deem an everyday activity, but it gave me such deep insight as to just how forceful the mind really is, and can somehow determine how far you can progress in life. It wasn't necessarily my physical strength that pushed me to do more because naturally 1 was tired and my body responded accordingly as signaled to my brain. It was more of my mental fortitude that kept me going because 1 had to reverse that conveyed message of tiredness to my brain, that it be turned into one of power. You can convince your mind what to believe and what your body should feel. That is why people hire personal trainers, coaches and mentors. They are there to convince your mind to push your body to greater limits; they deal with the mental blocks. Getting through a tough workout is not entirely your body physique, it is your mind convincing your body to keep going and that you can make it. From time to time you need to hear that voice urging you on that, "you can do it." You won't always have a personal trainer around you, but you can be your own encourager by elevating positive thoughts. So even through depression, frustration and adversity if you can just keep mentally strong, you can get through anything. You will break out in sweat and tears time and again but at the end of it all; you win!

You can convince your mind of anything and it soon adjusts to what you train it, that is why endurance and strength develop over time. For instance, at day one of going to the gym, your body may not be well adjusted to so much strain hence you begin with lifting the lowermost weights, and can stretch your work out time to about an hour. But by the time you get to day thirty, you're lifting weights which are twice the size of your initial mark and you are even sweating out for over an hour because your forbearance level has heightened. Training your mind works the same, at the onset of adversity you're stressed, depressed, and worry a lot. But as you begin to read the right material, be it the bible, self-help books or inspirational material; and as you pray with faith and learn to quickly reverse negative thoughts, you'll begin to notice that overtime you're less anxious, stronger and more hopeful. Changing your thought pattern is something that happens over time, it is part of the winning progression.

When you're faced with something whether it's a marathon or general life challenges, your body only caves in when your mind does. So, it's very possible to push yourself to limits you never believed you could. In this walk-through life you have the command to say, "I know it's hard but I can go on, I know I lost everything but I can recover from this, I know I'm in debt but I can be financially free. My life may not look anything like it right now but I shall be great." As you do so, you are subconsciously building your faith and it's only

WHY I NEVER GAVE UP

natural that your life in turn responds to your positivity. Sometimes you are your greatest motivator, by that l mean you can speak to your mind, let it always be things that are upright. Do not let negative thoughts run ahead of you, because in some moments that is exactly what happens. You can find yourself preplanning undesirable things that have not even happened, and when it turns out positive you realize how much time you wasted worrying about it. This shows that we have more control over our minds than we perceive.

The focus should be on empowering your mind, because you withstand what you're are mentally equipped for. When you are mentally prepared for something, it won't overwhelm you. It could be trying to build in a failing economy, developing a career, dealing with setbacks, ailing businesses or whatever it is you may be trying to leap over. If you mind is resilient nothing can weigh you down, you will have bad days but they will not cut you down. You may stumble, but you will always find a way to rise from it.

Trials can be interruptions to positive thinking, they weigh you down, distract and deter you and it always appears as, "nobody understands but you." People often give up when they think or feel isolated and that what they are going through, is only happening to them. How then do you keep a positive mind in the midst of adversity? What do you do when you feel your life has come to a complete stand still? When you're broken, depressed and downhearted but just can't talk about it? What do you do when you are engulfed in debt and everybody is calling you about the money owed to them, and you just don't know how you're going to pay it back? How do you cope in a marriage that's falling apart? What do you do when you don't have a college degree and everybody seems to be going ahead of you? When your career hasn't take off the way you hoped it would and you are so far behind? How do you keep your hope alive when you've been rejected and written off as a lost cause?

How do you recover from mistakes that almost cost you your life, and destiny? What do you do when you've been betrayed and your character has been wrecked? How do you go on after your divorce has just been finalized? What do you do when sickness hits your body and uttering a single word of prayer seems fruitless? How do you remain hopeful when you desire marriage but it seems to be wishful thinking? Maybe you're married but having children appears to be something you'll be denied of; how do you face each day?

How do you go through a season of being homeless and a basic meal is hard to come by? What do you do when those who promised to help you stop taking your calls? When you have absolutely nothing registered in your name, and your net worth is just but the clothes on your back? What about an individual who has just tragically lost a loved one? What of the orphan, not only left to raise herself but her siblings? What do you do when your life is such a clutter?

These are many of the trials that people try to cope with internally and sometimes behind closed doors. God said in John 16:33:

> *"In this world you will have tribulation, but be of good cheer l have overcome the world." (NKJV)*

He knew that challenges will come along the way but He gave a remedy. When He said he has overcome the world, He meant you too will overcome whatever trial you may encounter. Consequently, as delusional and unrealistic as it may sound, you can get out of any situation, you can recover and you can take your life back.

How do you overcome? You do so by renewing your mind daily to align with what God says, and all things positive. What you are experiencing and feeling is factual, but there is a truth of God that can offset every condition. It's a fact that you're broke but the truth is, all your needs are met in Christ. It's a fact that your heart is broken, but the Lord heals the brokenhearted and the peace will come. Maybe what you desire is humanly impossible but purpose that you'll be the miracle. The one who created this earth is supernatural and defies the laws science and nature, there is absolutely nothing He cannot do. If you can convince your mind to trust the truth more than the factual, your life can never be the same. Often when we haven't overcome, there is a truth we haven't discovered about our situation.

I wish l could tell you that all this can be done without great effort or difficulties, which would be very misleading. It will be strenuous sometimes and you will get frustrated but if you can endure, what's on the other side of adversity is much more beautiful. You have to see beyond where you currently are to be able to get out of that place of discomposure. Don't become comfortable with unideal circumstances, you have to see better for your life. It is my desire that this book serves as a reminder that you can capture your thoughts and counteract them with the positive no matter the situation or feelings, 2nd Corinthians 10:5 encourages us to make our thoughts submit to Christ.

"Fitting every loose thought and emotion and
impulse into the structure of a life shaped by Christ."
(MSG)

Seeing as God is a superior being, whose ideas are forever for your good and not the contrary, it will groom your mind to greatness. You can empower your mind so you too can begin to see a way out of anything.

I look at Nick Vujicic a man born without limbs but living life in fullness, inspiring and impacting nations in ways no one perceived. To be where he is, nothing in his physical form changed, but something within him did. He would let nothing hold him back and where other people may have seen misfortune, he saw purpose and fullness. He refused to be deterred by anything. What about Darrius Simmons the incredible pianist who plays so beautifully with just four fingers and presses the pedals with prosthetic legs? He has gone on to perform at the Carnegie hall, one of the most prestigious venues in the world for both classical and popular music. In his words "he wanted to inspire and put a smile on people's faces," and he did just that. He is a man defying odds and changing the world. What of those who came from poverty, but grew to be forerunners of wealth? I also think of the great Kenneth Hagin, born with a deformed heart, an incurable disease and was not expected to live? Against all odds he took God at his word and was completely healed and went on to share his testimony which birthed a ministry that impacted millions. What of Dana Johnson who was once homeless but by age twenty-three had made millions and became an author of several best-selling books?

I share these stories to show you that there is hope for you too but you have to believe that your life can be better despite the limitations that may threaten you. Begin to draw courage from what others have survived. What do you see in your present state? In your mind you can lean towards that "some people are so fortunate and blessed." Those thoughts that sideline you should not be given power, speak boldly about yourself and do not ever think fortune is only for a select few. Genuinely begin to believe that you too deserve better, in love, in health, in wealth, your career and every aspect of your life. You have to keep your hope alive and it begins with the way you think and perceive the world. Keep your thoughts in check, let them always align with the optimistic. Kenneth Hagin once said, "if it isn't positive then don't think about it."

I effectively learned how to apply that wisdom in my personal life and it brought me a long way. In whatever form you enter this world or whatsoever you may face ahead that may alter your life, always remember that God gives you the grace and ability to live an extraordinary life. Whether you are bankrupt, a single mother, or a divorcee, you can turn life's negatives into positives by changing the way you think.

WHY I NEVER GAVE UP

In my journey I've researched successful people who were once in the deep pit and they have one thing in common; they had to change the way they think. They had to realign their minds to that which is positive and thereafter, significant change followed in their lives. You too can be one among them, there's hope for you. When l won in my mind, l would still see things around me that were not desirable but chose not to be moved. Instead, I purposed that l was victorious and eventually it would manifest in the fullness of time. I would wake up and say l choose faith, I will not worry or dwell on the negative. When you've won in your mind, you have won in your life.

There's a sense in which positive thinking is grooming yourself into faith. It is because you actually start to believe that things will get better and the impossible can become a reality, and that no situation is a lifeless end. When you have a positive mindset, you begin to gain confidence that what you hope for, can in fact happen. I like to think of it as repairing your thinking, the discipline of not conforming to what life throws at you, but instead transforming your life by changing the way you think.

It changes within you before it changes around you.

God did not create you on his idle time or pretty much when he had run out of things to do. The same way that God cannot lie is the same way he cannot make a mistake. There was a reason and deliberate plan for your creation, never forget that it was a thought process. Use your valley lows and what seem like death moments to tap into the revelation of why you were put here on earth. Let your pain birth destiny.

I DISCOVERED PURPOSE

————————·•❧•·————————

By the time you read this book I will be a published author, it means I discovered my purpose. My life hasn't been without distractions and detours, there was a time my image was far from the woman I am today, and it all began with getting pregnant soon after high school. The last thing any parent wants to hear is that their teenage daughter is welcoming a child into this world. How was a child going to take care of another? I could see the devastation and disappointment in their eyes and so I would spend the next coming years trying to redeem myself. In the kind of society I grew up in, I had stripped myself of every opportunity in flourishing, and according to what was generally believed, I had also missed out on a career and marriage. Even though I was a teen mom, the first-time I laid my eyes on my daughter, I felt a sense of compassion towards her, she was just so precious and innocent. Her innocence in it all, is what really pierced my heart, I couldn't help but love her.

I soaked in the moments of motherhood but nothing could have prepared me for the years of dysfunction that I would live through as l sought to find myself and get onto the path any parent would have desired for their children. For years l struggled, especially with trying to unravel why God put me on this earth. l was that girl constantly in the shadows, the one you write off, the least likely to succeed, the one who watched others graduate and get married. I was the girl in the background cheering others on, yet having no understanding as to what direction my life was taking. I felt invisible, as if the world couldn't see who l really was and what l had to offer. I too wanted to say "mama l made it" but life seemed to be for everybody else but me, going with the flow soon became what l conformed to but; "that wasn't the dream."

As l matured especially in my relationship with God the eyes of my understanding began to open. I knew l wanted more for my life, but didn't know how to get to my desired place. Sure enough, it took so much blood sweat and tears to get to it. It was not until l experienced the worst heartbreak of my entire life that my heart became the ultimate sacrifice and, in the process, brought forth a whole new woman.

One afternoon in my season of healing l sat on my bed reading through the bible about the story of Joseph, and oddly as l did so, it felt as though l was reading about myself. Life had battered him so hard and he had dealt with some of life's worst. He was broken, betrayed, hurt, embarrassed, mocked, taunted but his story ended in honor, vindication, glory and led to the liberation of so many others. So, here l am reading this fascinating story when a good friend of mine messages just to check if I'm doing alright. As we are chatting he says to me "remember you are special and made for an assignment that is unique." By then I'm almost moved to tears and he continues to say, "God is a God of purpose, look at Joseph and what he went through but it was a set up for God to fulfill purpose."

How could he have possibly known that I had been reading about the story of Joseph? To even text me at that precise moment left me in so much awe of God. This was His confirmation to me that I had a purpose and everything I went through was not in vain, and he sent a friend to settle that truth. My pain was going to help others heal and liberate them. No experience was going to go to waste, it would all fulfill purpose.

Most of us have been in that place where life pounds us harshly that people can barely recognize us, and we too begin to question our very own existence. Moments where you genuinely feel God must have surely made a serious oversight when He created you. It's natural to feel that way when going through adversities but find comfort in knowing that God is not in the business of creating things for idleness, He does so with a plan and a purpose. Ever notice the way a mother solemnly prepares for an unborn baby so that at its arrival all is beautifully organized? The nursery, the color coordination of the clothes, the stacked nappies and blankets are all prearranged? That is how God sets up for our place here on earth, He prepares way in advance a life and path to walk in. This is enlightened in Ephesians 2:10:

"For we are His workmanship created in Christ Jesus for good works, which God prepared beforehand that we should walk in them." (NKJV)

God creates a path, but the enemy puts obstacles on it such that people become clouded about what their purpose truly is, or even if they have one for that matter. Particularly when their life doesn't reflect what they hoped it would. Maybe your life hasn't been entirely perfect and has somehow dealt you a harsh hand, but know that in God's terminology, there is no mistake.

I did not discover my purpose till l was thirty-one, prior to that I had moments where l would cry before God and tell him I was tired and life was just so hard, I was exhausted, burned out and couldn't understand why l was still existing. But the moment I did, it gave me a sense of something to live for. I discovered hidden strengths and abilities l never even knew l carried. It is in my brokenness that l discovered purpose, in the midst of what seemed to be end of me. Who would have ever imagined that this girl who was a teen mom and missed out on an opportunity to go to university could write a book? For me to get ahead was something unthinkable, I was that girl you overlook but when I aligned with purpose, everything else began to fall into place.

So anytime you feel weighed down by life always remember that, there is a Father who put you here on earth to pour out and dispense the virtuous things He placed on the inside of you. Things that will change the world and give hope to many. No matter the scope or magnitude, everybody has a role on earth in their respective lives. Be it teachers, cashiers, doctors, lawyers, pastors, drivers or nurses, do what you do with the utmost excellence. Never give in and when it seems there's nothing left to live for, let purpose be your saving grace and reason to go on when you don't feel like it anymore. You just may have not discovered it yet, but it's already within you. The fulfillment that comes with pursuing purpose is undeniable. Until you discover what you were put here on earth for, you'll be content with the status quo.

Spend time with the one who authored your life, He will whisper into your ear, things you could have never uncovered in your own strength. There is a life He predestined for you to walk in, dig deeper till you find it, you too are of value to this world. You were created for good; but you cannot discover purpose outside of Him who created you.

Positive affirmation: Say out audibly; "I was created for good, I have a purpose."

I PUT GOD FIRST

———— ••❧•• ————

D on't let anybody delude you, a life void of Christ is empty. You'll get the businesses, cars, money, marriage, houses but still be so unfilled. The complicated issue with success or a life not founded on God is that, it is not full circle or complete. You can be a millionaire but feel as though something is still missing within you. That is why people then run to other factors to fill that unexplainable void they'll be feeling.

Because of it, some even turn to illicit acts, fleeting thrills and excessive indulgence to compensate for something that is lacking within them.

You will stop being envious of anyone the day you realize that in gaining the world many have lost the core of their being. It is futile to gain every material thing you can possibly imagine but be empty in spirit; there should be a balance. God's idea of life and good success is to be fulfilled spirit, soul and body. This is echoed in the following scriptures:

Mark 8:36- "What good would it do to get everything you want and lose you, the real you?" (MSGE)

3 John:2 - "Beloved, I pray that you may prosper in all things and be in health, just as your soul prospers." (NKJV)

The unsurpassed order of things is putting God first because what is then founded on Him, is in turn sustained by Him. Build your business, build your career, marriage and legacy but let the evident hand in it all, be God. What you build your life on determines its longevity and sustenance, you need a firm foundation of Christ for the imperfect world we live in hence everything should begin with Him. Matthew 6:33 is a verse many have heard numerous times, it narrates:

"Seek the kingdom of God above all else and live righteously, and He will give you everything you need." (NLT)

When God said this, it wasn't to imply that the things you desire are farfetched, it was to set a principle that He should be the driving force and foundation of your life. When you build in a world where the upright order of things was compromised there is a foundation of Christ that is needed, apart from that you build on unsteady ground. He wanted you to be blessed in wholeness lacking nothing, He desired that your spirit, soul and body be in fullness.

In my journey I came to a place where my heart grew most sincere towards God and I truly desired Him more than anything. I stopped living a passive life and openly submitted to God. As I sought Him wholeheartedly, I watched Him arrange my life in ways that humbled and left me in awe. He picked me up from the wreckage and put me in my place of prominence; from oblivion to an author. He also began to show me what my purpose entailed and how to map my vision. In His plan for my life He had already established that I would be an author but for many years I did not know that. The moment it was revealed to me the means to go about it became available, and the ability to do it well was cultivated. With that came the resources and skills to make it all a reality. I learned and researched on what it took to be an author, the ideologies of what it is to proofread, edit, format and publish a book; I became smarter and technical.

God holds everything you need pertaining to life, when you get a hold of Him, know that the things you've ever needed will begin to materialize. When you put Him first He cares that you are whole, clothed, covered, taken care of and liberated. He cares that you are successful and every need is met. Life may have its challenges, but it's all the harder without God. Thrive to put Him first in everything regarding your life, and watch Him add the extraordinary to it. When you honor God, you've put yourself on a path to purpose and destiny.

I never gave up because I put God first, and He became my redemption. Who are you putting first?

PART 2

GOD HEALED MY HEART

————··✦✦✦··————

I'm certainly no expert, but the downfall of many has been relationships. The struggle to get it right in love has left scores with deep wounds and scars. People come out of relationships looking like they have just come out of a sword fight- "panting and bleeding."

Adversity comes in different forms, mine came in that of a heartbreak. If you've ever experienced overwhelming distress, you will understand that the crushing will wreck you to your knees. As I've observed heartbreak is one such thing that can completely ravish a person. This is one that forever changed me.

Before l was the woman l am today, l got into a relationship with the wrong man and it would later rip me to shreds. Initially we had met a few years back but would only date at a later stage. From the few things l knew about him I could sense he wasn't right for me because he was the total opposite of who l was. I was your typical Christian girl and he was unruly, a heavy drinker, lived a carefree and casual life, basically we were unequally yoked. He was the kind that argued and questioned if the bible was real because it was written by men and downright refused to go to church because in his words "he's not going to sit and listen to somebody telling him what to do." He always said he would live his life the best way he sees it. This is not even the saddest part, the most devastating is, I still went on to date him even after having gotten a glimpse of that side of him. It is a shame for me to admit that. I knew better, but at the time I did not love myself enough or have the self-esteem to shut off such inexcusable things.

Have you ever noticed how we are all a little intelligent till it comes to love? For some strange reason it's as if the brain has a major malfunction and your mental acumen just disappears into the radar. You can be a professor at Harvard university, a lawyer or doctor but put together in one room with someone who never went to school, the logic and intellect on love seems to be just the same; we fall hard......

Alike to most relationships ours was first founded on a friendship. During that period, it took me a while to open up to him about my personal life because of the nature of his character, deep down in my heart my gut feeling prompted that he wasn't good for me, but I suppressed it. When I would post pictures of my daughter on social media or put her as my display picture on other communication platforms he would say nothing. When we finally did speak about her, I got the backlash I expected for having a child and possessing the personality I did. Prior to us dating I was on a journey of

31

celibacy and truly wanted to honor God with my life, but he would always get agitated and harshly say that I could not have such high standards because I'm not a virgin anymore and I have a child. In his eyes I was undeserving of certain things especially purity, value and high regard because I was a mother. He would also say relations are what the body needs and would talk me out of chastity and tell me to stop making innocent people pay for what other men did to me in the past. I cannot count the number of times I've heard that misguided statement. In his mind my celibacy was a punishment to other men that wanted to be with me.

Especially because I had a child, his attitude towards me slowly changed, he spoke to me anyway he felt, was disrespectful and in one incident implied that I was showing too much eagerness for a relationship. I couldn't understand how that even made any sense because I was the one holding him to a higher standard. What he intensely disliked was the fact that I insisted on carrying myself as a woman of value yet in his eyes I wasn't deserving of it. We would argue so much because I just wouldn't give in until one day it escalated to a point where he stopped talking to me and shut me out completely. I let it go and focused on being a better woman but a couple of months later; he resurfaced.

This time he proclaimed that he was a changed man, was drinking less and even considering to stop. He determinedly held the words that he was done with games and ready to settle down with a good woman and felt 1 was the right one, I suddenly went from unworthy, to one who is of high regard . He also strongly expressed how he was ready to commit and we spoke about marriage and the future. Surprisingly he also seemed to have warmed up to my having a child and made mention of us being one happy family someday. As everything progressed there were a few occasions where he was supportive and sacrificial but it would all be shortlived. Even though we had argued about church in the past, this time he promised that he would attend and take one for the team. Of course, he later never kept his word because he wanted nothing to do with it. Our beginning was not the sweetest, he had his moments of being kind and caring but when he wanted to be inhuman, he really was. At times he said all the right things and 1 was so convinced that we would make it because he had promised to always be loyal. Those short moments of him showing kindness is what 1 held onto, but when he finally had me in his life, everything took a turn for the worst.

As the relationship grew he didn't want to be questioned when he was wrong, nor did he want accountability, he wanted to live like he was single. As each day passed, it unveiled who he was in truth. He was emotionally and verbally abusive at times, the kind that wasn't afraid to throw profanities around and show you inappropriate hand gestures when he was angry. He would sternly say things such as he doesn't care whether you're a man old enough to be his father, if you dare cross his path he will show you the hand slur. Even before we became official I saw the outbursts of anger, on one occasion I asked him about a promise he had made and he became so angry and sent me a message laced with bad words, I was speechless. He only wanted to do things at his own time and when he felt like it. He delivered based on his mood.

After a while I began to see the disinterest and inconsistencies. His excuse of being that way was, he did not want to rush anything of which yet again made no sense because I was the one calling for things to be done the upright way. When problems arose, he would shift the blame on me for rushing everything. After our very first misunderstanding he spoke words that crushed me, he said my showing devotion to love and commitment, was a turn off to him. This was after I had questioned him on the distance he was creating between us. Nothing of what he said to that effect had any logic in it. Was commitment not a prerequisite for a successful relationship? He was ever so verbal about loyalty, was that not it? Being a good woman to this man didn't earn me love, it earned me contempt.

One of the things that also came as a shock was his tendency of smoking weed, I was not aware of it till we were officially together. Naturally I did put forward my concerns to him about it but he would always justify himself with the excuse that its quite normal because CEOs use it habitually. This to me was something l could not possibly live with, I wasn't holding him accountable for things he did as a teenager, but for what he carried all the way into adulthood. For somebody who was almost reaching forty, l expected better from him. I thought he was focused, knew what he wanted and was a man of integrity. He had grown in age but hadn't matured.

As if that wasn't upsetting enough he was already chatting up a female colleague and telling her l wasn't his girl after that first disagreement. He was even planning a getaway vacation with yet another woman. I knew that if this was the way he handled conflict, l was in trouble. When l asked him about it, his response was he didn't want the little birdies to fly seeing that we were fighting and things were not working out between us. He had something to fall back on and wasn't committed to me, l was never his priority. My understanding of a solid relationship was to get rid of baggage before moving on to something new, he believed in getting right only within the relationship after a test run. He pointed out how l had traits of his previous partner and that he was having second thoughts about me because he could see trouble coming. I soon caught on to the fact that in our seasons of being single whilst l was getting whole and growing, he was filling voids with women, weed and liquor. So, his first instinct was to go back to those things when all was amiss.

I saw the red flags before things spiraled out of control but somehow thought it would get better. In my case for whatever reason, 1 thought 1 could pray him into a better man and convince him to go to church, 1 wanted to turn him into my ideal gentleman. I would ask God to soften his heart so he would agree to go to church, but it proved effortless. Life continued and, in some moments, he tried to show love where he could but it was all based on how he felt at that particular time. He had two extremes, he could be extremely nice and extremely ruthless, there was no middle ground. Nonetheless, 1 put all my energy into being nothing like his ex because he was so vocal on how she had trust issues. 1 worked so hard to make sure 1 wasn't anything like the other woman that 1 soon forgot that it would never work with the wrong man. I cooked, cleaned, did laundry, ironed and prayed for him, especially his career and for God to favor him. 1 broke my celibacy journey to win over a man who would later break me to a point where 1 couldn't imagine anything better than death.

Things took a turn for the worst when 1 found out about an affair he had with a married woman, I would have never known about her had she not been calling so much. Before the truth would surface, out of concern 1 did let him know that for someone who is married, she called a bit much. As predicted he told me what I wanted to hear, "she's just a friend." He assured me that he was good friends with her husband as well and even pulled out his phone to show me pictures of the couple on social media which I found very odd. I could discern that he was lying and I would soon uncover the truth.

As the truth began to unfold he had no choice but to come clean. The communication between them was so blunt and left no room for confusion or doubt, it showed the character of man he really was. The woman did not seem to have much moral sense of right or wrong either because she would ask him if he had any last words so she could cover her tracks from her husband. They showered each other with affection and spoke about how much they missed each other, all the sweet and overt talk. When I confronted him about it he detailed that it was in the past now though the woman was ready to leave her husband for him, but he declined because he did not want to take on the responsibility of her children. But because of the way I found out, he told me I had broken the trust in the relationship and I was disloyal. Somehow, he managed to flip everything over and point toward that it was my fault for finding out so I hurt myself, "reverse psychology." He went on to say I had issues, but I was confused because I was the sober minded one. Before long he had told so many people and anybody who cared to listen that I was a problem. I was now known as the woman with a questionable character, he made me look like I was unhinged.

From that day on things were never the same. He told me I could never be trusted and I've got issues just like his ex, this would be the beginning of an inferno I was never ready for. The affair was one thing, but the even bigger issue was that the woman's first-born child, was supposedly his. They had spoken about DNA testing and he had professed to her that they will always be unfinished business. At the beginning of our relationship when things were fairly ok between us, we opened up to each other about our biggest fears. It was just a random question about what we both fear the most. Shockingly his was, he feared being made to raise a child that was not his own. I couldn't quite make out the meaning of the statement when he said it but when things began to emerge, it became clear that he knew there was deep secret buried in his heart. Another man was possibly raising his child and it soon became his worst anxiety.

Given everything that was happening we were still not officially separated. So, at one-point we had a discussion as I tried to reason with him about the child situation. I advised him that whatever he decided to do, it should be at the best interest of the child. He openly affirmed that even if they did confirm he was the father, they had agreed that it was a secret they would both take to the grave. In disbelief I asked him why he would rob an innocent child of the truth and a chance to know her real father? I was unprepared for what he would say next, his reaction was "do you have any idea what child support will do to me and my finances?" I was shaken, he continued to say the truth was best kept a secret for the sake of all families involved. The more I pressed on the issue the more I infuriated him. Him being so spoken about how much he loves kids, was just empty talk. There is no way he would have ever fully accepted my child had things worked out between us. For the way I discovered the truth about him he put it across that he would hold it against me forever. I had awakened the monster in him and he was going to make me pay severely for it. I was never supposed to find out such deep truths about him.

From then on, the emotional and verbal abuse worsened. My heart bled one particular day when he sat across the room, looked me straight in the eye and told me he did not want me in his life anymore but still wanted my body. Yes, he said it "he just wanted my body." I don't know what was worse, him telling me that, "at least he was being honest" or the fearlessness to actually say something as demeaning as that to me. Who was this man? In his eyes I was worth nothing, he viewed me as an object to be tossed around and not given any dignity. I was a body to be used to fulfill his selfish desires. He would laugh in my face and say I must be living under a rock for thinking people can't have fun with their bodies, he said it was normal and I should; "live a little." There are things he said without realizing how damaging they are to a woman and her self-esteem. Couldn't he have at least protected my fragile heart instead of making it so apparent how worthless he thought I was? Nothing could have armed me for me all his.

When all this drama was unfolding I was in the process of finding my feet. I wasn't financially well-adjusted and one day he said to me, I was such a one who just wants to be fed. He used cuss words to tell me how I was a grown woman and that I could figure things out on my own. He belittled and dishonored me so much, in his eyes I was a nobody. I remember how little I felt, but I knew deep down God had planted great things on the inside of me and that it was just a matter of time before they manifested. Never in this lifetime had anyone ever made me feel so small as though I didn't matter.

Before some of the fights intensified I had a conversation with him about God and I was alluding to the fact that, the Lord does speak to people. He burst out laughing and said I should never say something like that out loud, because I'll be taken to a psychiatric hospital. My heart sank, in his eyes I was a lunatic for saying God speaks and believing in Him. I had never met a man who resented and mocked God the way he did. We would argue for hours as I tried to defend my faith yet he strove to make me look foolish. He wanted to drag me down with him.

And this wasn't all, he would chat up that married woman and tell her how I've got issues and she would advise him to get rid of me and that he should have never been with me in the first place. She called my actions stupid and told him she was worried that I now knew too much and could possibly reach out to her husband and everything would blow up. Not once did he stand up for me, instead he told her not to worry and assured her that he will always have her back and will definitely get rid of me and they laughed about it. I watched them laugh and plot to get rid of me before I cause any trouble. Moments later he would ask if he could see her. Yes, they were still being sneaky. It was so hurtful but comforting to know that I wasn't crazy after all, he was not a principled man. He was willing to chase after a married woman but would never try to be civil towards a good woman. Everything he denied me of, he was willing to give to another woman, and not just any but a married one. Loyalty, respect and care she got it all. He was a man who preached loyalty so much and always maintained that we should never allow anyone to speak ill of either of us in our absence yet in reality, he was the most treacherous person.

I knew it would never stop, because their relationship stemmed from way back. According to him they were "cool like that" and have always had a flirty relationship even though she was married. What bewildered me was how he would seek advice about our relationship from a married woman he had an affair with. How was that reasonable? He would drool over her pictures on social media, his like never came up short. I saw the way he gazed at her picture when he scrolled through social media in moments he thought I wouldn't notice. That kind of pause that a man takes to look at a woman he wishes he could have; it was heart crushing. I cannot explain the sinking feeling of knowing that you're not the one, that you didn't make the cut and weren't enough. That there is nothing you could have done different to be finally considered and valued.

Because I now knew so much respect became a rare thing, he would call his friends in plain sight of me and laugh out loud on the phone over how I was a worse trade in than his ex and how he now longed for the past, all the subliminal guy talk. I'm not sure why I still bothered to confront him because I was always met with a fit of rage, he would say he could speak to whoever he wanted. Confrontation was an attack to him; his anger was unexplainable and he did not want to be called out on anything. In one instance I specifically asked him why he sees absolutely nothing wrong in himself because everything he said about his ex, was what he was beginning to say about me; "we all had issues." He had once mentioned that she had so many problems such that she was attending therapy of which 1 wasn't completely convinced that was the truth, it seemed overplayed given his borderline character. He began to say all women are the same so clearly, he saw nothing wrong within him. Everybody else was the problem, he saw fault in everyone but him.

I couldn't understand why he would make those kinds of remarks considering that he was making no effort to be a better man. He desired things from other people that he wasn't willing to give. He wanted loyalty but was the worst at being trusted. When 1 would confront him about all the other issues we were having, 1 would always be met with so much rage and he would allege that I'm nothing to him to question what he does, its his life and he will bear the consequences. One time he said 1 should ask him why he didn't feel guilty about having an affair with a married woman, 1 couldn't comprehend why that was even a question? He had such strange rhetoric. In all the fighting he would say things such as, I'm in his way of being with other women and once we are apart he can have his way. Having been with him proved to be taking a stroll with the enemy. He was a narcissist and when you date one, you're dating someone void of a conscience and sensitivity, he was a vile person.

Whilst he was doing all he desired 1 turned to prayer, it's what 1 knew to do when things were not right. My plea was more of what can 1 change in me for him, I blamed myself for everything. What I did not realize at the time was that 1 needed to stop looking for answers, concerning something I knew was not ordained by God. I wanted God to bless my sin, I wanted to force his hand on my compromise. I wanted him to understand that relationships weren't an easy breeze for people like me. Ones with children outside of wedlock and because of that, l couldn't do things the way He required. If l had known how much it was going to destroy me, l would have run for my dear life.

Picture being hurt by someone who everyone holds in high respect, it makes you look untruthful. Only l knew who he really was behind closed doors. He told me l had it good with him and that I was ungrateful and should have let things slide than to untangle them, and even question him about it. He further said l bring out the worst in him and how l was the type of woman who wanted a fairytale. I actually didn't want one, l just wanted something that is authentic, I desired better for me. Amongst other things, he mentioned that l had ruined my chances with him; he said it like he was the prize.

I was also aware of the fact that he was spending money on female colleagues buying lunch for them, but l was not worth one single date. I never got the flowers and the thoughtful gifts, l was the girl who washed dishes and did laundry. With time l did ask him about it and as usual he burst out laughing and said l should take him out on a date too. He had this cruel laugh that could shatter your core and it was strange that he would gust out in laughter in the middle of serious conversations. In those moments he seemed to be outside of character and the normal, I figured it was partly because of the weed because nobody in their upright state would do or say the things he did. For somebody who had been using it for years he had developed a dependency on it. To be happy he needed weed, to sleep he needed weed, he couldn't function normally anymore without it. He had disclosed to me that he had also tried drugs in the past and based on his dysfunction and disorientation, 1 couldn't rule out the fact that he would from time to time revert to them when no one was watching. Weed and drugs are all fun and games till you've suffered at the hands of a man who is controlled by it and can't be clearheaded without it. That's where he derived his balance, joy and peace from, women came as an added extra package.

He had fits of fury, strange talk and things you wouldn't ordinarily hear from a rational person, he seemed to have two personalities. His regular atmosphere was outbursts of anger, unpredictable behavior and odd dialogue. As somebody who smoked weed he would laugh out so loudly and tell me that the woman he will end up with will smoke like he does. His peculiarity showed even in general conversations, his views were mostly negative. He held a belief in his mind that men should enjoy their younger years, live recklessly, associate with as many women before they marry so that when they are finally ready to settle down, they will be so burned out. This meant they wouldn't have missed out on anything and therefore commit by reason of that. This would also warrant for faithfulness in their marriage. He would even say he sees nothing wrong with flirting to close a business deal, and would allow his wife to do it as long as it brought food to the table. I could not wrap my head around his principles that lacked integrity.

Occasionally he would invite me to join him when he had a smoke. Some days 1 would contemplate on drinking and smoking weed with him, maybe then he would find me interesting and love me right; 1 thought 1 was boring to him. The only thing that stopped me is the fact that conforming would have been failing him because my idea of love, was to make each other better. I tried to be the woman who won him over with a calm and gentle spirit, 1 prayed to be a better woman for him but nothing changed. It's as if the more 1 prayed the more 1 aggravated him. I had my flaws but 1 was a good woman, he wanted somebody to drink and smoke with, and 1 just wasn't that person. He would often say we are just too different.

My heart sank each day, 1 had been hurt in the past but nothing like this. My sin was uncovering things 1 should never have, and automatically it made me the worst woman on the planet in his eyes. One day I reached out to him in an effort to try and understand why he was treating me so badly and he

46

said to me, "people get hurt all the time, so I'll get over it." I was devastated. Those were the words of a wounded man with unresolved issues, I plead for sympathy but received none. In another incident he passed a comment that, l was at his mercy and should just suck it up whether l was happy or unhappy about the way he was treating me. This man couldn't have possibly given me what l deserved.

It made me become fully aware of the element that what people are hurt with, is what they deny others of. It could be love, loyalty or anything good. Just because they didn't receive it, they feel everyone else doesn't deserve it either. When you're broken, you love from your brokenness. Whatever emotion you haven't dealt with is what you draw love from. In one instance he had told me he wasn't sure of what he wanted and if you're uncertain about somebody you won't commit, you will give bits and pieces just to keep the relationship going. He was a broken man hurting other people because he was hurt.

The psychological trauma was real, l began to sink into depression. This man broke the deep rooted nature of my being, l thought l was going to lose my mind...

During that period, I told him I had so much regret for compromising for him and that l would start over, this time with God. With the uppermost confidence he said to me, l would never find a man willing to be celibate and that no guy could put up with that unless he was of my character. As common he laughed as he said it, to him my expectations were deranged. One thing I could never understand is why a man will disturb a woman's peace only to later destroy her. He promises her the world but later falters. Though it is true that nothing is forced because each individual always has a choice on who they allow into their hearts, but why the contemptibility? What pleasure do you derive from seeing someone hurt and bleeding?

I was tired of dysfunctional relationships. I always seemed to get the bitter end of the stick, I left relationships broken, empty and bitter. Where was I getting it wrong? I too wanted to be valuable to somebody. I was so broken that I vowed to never feel that pain again. What made this heartache different, was that it challenged my faith. In the past I had never been made to feel senseless for believing in God. What hurt even more is that, one of the people I confided in who I thought was a friend, later turned on me. She too began to discredit and speak ill of me but I kept silent and did not confront her. She would sympathize with me and say she would pray for me, but later became an unfamiliar person. I knew I was done for the day I spoke to her over the phone and her words and tone had changed, pointing to the direction that it was all my fault and I'm the one with issues not that man. Even after I found out that she had turned on me she still continued to say she was praying for me. I didn't know if I could trust anyone, I became cautious about who I vent to.

Had I been a woman with a healthy self-image I wouldn't have allowed certain things to happen in my life. But because the relationship with myself was not where it needed to be, I allowed people to treat me horribly. I didn't believe I was worth so much more than I put out myself to be. In my life, I had seen it all, physical and emotional abuse. As my relationship with this man drew to a close, he erupted in laughter in front of me one peculiar day and said, "even after knowing all this you still wanted to be with me?" His laughter pierced my soul. How could somebody be so cold-hearted? I thought I was being patient but he interpreted it as foolishness.

Reality hit me hard, I began to blame myself for everything, maybe it really was my fault and I should have just kept silent and been the submissive girlfriend. I found myself apologizing for not accepting the worst from him. I went on a guilt trip till I had a moment of clarity that made me say, but wait a minute; this person is very abusive, inhuman, spiteful, irresponsible, selfish, shows no empathy and is unapologetic. He was making me pay for having expectations that were within reason. Honesty, loyalty and faithfulness should have been the bare minimum but it a was a nag to him. I realized that I should have taken him seriously when he said to me, "I shouldn't have any expectations, but just go with the flow." He was that type of man with no principles or integrity. I thought 1 was being sensible because 1 would have never asked him for what 1 wasn't willing to give.

How was 1 going to survive all this? How could somebody possibly go through all this and remain the same? It was just too much. When he found me, 1 was in such a good place. I was growing and content in God but when he left, 1 was a shattered pile of desolation. It didn't help that he was so cunning, around other people he played the victim. The select few that knew him really well were those he smoked and drank with.

As fate would have it, we went our separate ways; but the torture never stopped. He accused me of taking pictures of him smoking weed and circulating them. That wasn't even reasonable, it was so strange and absurd. I was out of his life but he was still tormenting me, he wanted to shame me in the eyes of everyone so he wouldn't feel so guilty about the way he treated me. One of the things he loathed when we were still together was that 1 spoke up about his wrong doing. He would say he hates being questioned so my having a voice passed off as disrespect to him. I had to be silent and take all the kicks laying on the ground. To the bitter end, he showed no remorse or regret for anything, even when 1 enquired about the deceitful accusations.

I think of how harsh the healing process was, we were done but he was still in my head. I could hear him laughing, mocking, taunting and belittling me. The little self-esteem 1 had, went straight out the window. I still carried the things he said and did to me, 1 did not realize how severe the damage was, till 1 was out of his life. For the first couple of days 1 could barely sleep because 1 was still troubled and weighed down by the things he said to me. His words deeply scarred me and my feelings were that of being on the losing side. The painful reminders, regrets and self-condemnation beat me to a pulp.

Because he had challenged my faith quite a lot, 1 had so many moments of thinking; "maybe I'm too much of a Christian, and 1 should tone it down." He made me feel so terrible about it, and always tried to talk me out of it. He made me look thoughtless and despised anything to do with God, his effort was to pull me away. I had so much anger in me and it was hurting my disposition, stressing my health and stealing my peace. The anger felt like something heavy sitting on my chest. I became so vengeful and considered hurting him too. I thought of making his worst nightmare a reality by making the affair a known thing to those he feared the most, but my heart wouldn't let me. It took everything in me to get up and face each day. I could come up with a million excuses as to why 1 got into a relationship with a toxic person but the state of things as they actually are is that, we always have a choice.

Things could have turned out completely different had 1 chosen a different path, and because 1 didn't, 1 paid brutally for it. His behavior was totally unacceptable and inexcusable but I could have saved myself by using wisdom instead of emotions. This is where emotional intelligence becomes a crucial part of an individual's life. I wasn't sure if I would make it, I would cry before the Lord and tell him I'm beyond broken, wounded and I need Him to personally come down and do something or speak a word that will save my life.

Part of my journey to healing comprised of accepting what had happened. I couldn't change what was done but could face what lay ahead with an attitude that my life will get better. What had happened was excruciating but acceptance is one of the first steps to healing, its understanding that you can heal and there is life after heartbreak. I also had to accept that my path was different, unconventional relationships may have worked for other people but would never work for me. It would have never aligned with my destiny, it was either God's way or no way. I spent time in the word of God and also read books and healing material. The only counsel I had was that of the Holy Spirit. Worship also got me through that season, there is something about it that makes you hope again despite what may be going on around you. It gives you a sense of comfort that there's a higher power ready to turn things around for you; it uplifts your spirit. So, each day I would lay before the Lord and weep, I would tell him I wasn't sure if I was going to survive this. I was tired and beat down, I needed supernatural strength. Some days I would wail so loud that I feared the neighbors would hear me, but I had to release the pain.

I wept for the kind of world our daughters are born into, I bled for every woman who has ever gone through what I did. I told God that I couldn't wait to see other women become whole because I wanted to use my pain for good, I cried out to him for wisdom. When you know what it feels like to be broken beyond acceptance, the last thing you want to see is another broken person. It turned into something so personal for me, my heart posture became one of desiring to serve others for their good. One of those healing season days when I was so overwhelmed by everything, I fell on my knees and began to cry, I thought I was going to utter words of agony as I usually did before God but instead, I found myself saying, "thank you for loving me," He had rescued me from a lifetime of torment. I thanked God for ending that relationship, something I had never done before in the past. There was something about this heartbreak that I conceived had thrown me right into my position of purpose and destiny. That man thought he was tossing me away but he threw me right into destiny.

God heard my cry and He began to show me how to get out of my adversity. He strengthened my heart and gave me assurance that this wasn't the end. It's in those moments that He spoke to me about who I really was and showed me the kind of future He desired for me. The things I had been chasing after for so long were far from what he sought for me, l had been short changing myself. All l ever needed was right in front of my eyes but l chased down things that eventually destroyed me and made me sorrowful. As l healed I was about to embark on a journey that would not only change my life, but that of many others. What was meant to destroy me, He was going to turn into a story of victory. I was led to study in depth the story of Joseph in the bible and God confirmed that my story would end in honor, vindication and greatness. Everything that the enemy intended to destroy me with God would use and turn it around for my good, it would change many lives especially those of women. Genesis 50 vs 20 says:

you plotted evil against me, but God turned it into something good in order to preserve the lives of many people. (GNT)

I made it, not only for myself but for many others, years from now people will read this book and not give up. God loved me so much that he came for me, l went against His will, but He still came for me. As l reflected on my past l truly began to see things differently, those who saw me as troublesome were people l dated, but those who knew me well, saw a decent and humble person. In that moment l understood what l needed to change, and that was the character of men l let into my heart.

Just after my separation from that man l happened to have a conversation with a stranger l met in a public facility and he said to me, "there's a peace about you it's comforting." I was stirred to tears because he said it at a time l felt l was most broken. I had just come out of a relationship where l was so used to being mistreated and being told I'm nothing but trouble. Where l was constantly told I've got issues and because of me, all women are the same. How was it even possible that somebody who didn't even know me that well could see beyond the walls?

In that moment l had divine understanding that the man God has for you, will speak to the woman that you had no idea was hidden in you. He will see beyond the canvas of your heart and have a revelation of who you truthfully are. He will see beyond the things that stained your heart, the past hurt, betrayals, mistakes and failures. Where others saw war, he will see peace. Where some may have seen brokenness, he will see wholeness. He will not see you as a burden but a comfort. Where another man saw trouble, he will see refinement. He will see something in you that other men could never see all along. His words will heal and not tear down, he will evoke peace, strength and awaken the beauty hidden in you. He will see your scars as a mark of strength, not weakness or something to prey on, or make a mockery of. He will make you love, love. Because he has a revelation of who you are, he will vow to protect your sanctuary and preserve your purity.

Have you ever wondered why some men treated you so badly in the past yet deep down you knew you're such a good woman? It is because they did not have a revelation of who you are, if they did, they would have treated you better. That gave me so much peace and closure.

I never saw that stranger again but those words were inscribed in my heart because God reminded yet again that l was truly special and in the fullness of time the right man would come along. One morning when l woke up, God led to pray for my future partner. As l was praying and thanking Him that he is a man of integrity, kindness and love He whispered to my heart, "he looks just like Me." I smiled and I knew that God wasn't referring to his features, but his heart and character. That beautiful moment taught me that the man God has for any woman will be so much like Him in character. He will be faithful, loving, kind, honest, sincere, and patient. In essence he will have the fruits of the Spirit. If you've ever asked, "how will l know if he's the one?" You will know him by his fruits. Galatians 5:22-23 reads:

> *"But the Holy Spirit produces this kind of fruit in our lives: love, joy, peace, patience, kindness, goodness, faithfulness, gentleness and self-control." (NLT)*

When a man walks into your life, ask yourself; is he kind, patient, faithful, gentle and does he have self-control? That is how you will know if "he's the one."

As l continued to heal, I still had my weak moments but held on and found comfort in God. I would feel the pain arising but whisper to myself that, "I'm going to be alright, this too shall pass and my heart will heal." I learned to trust and worship God when l had nothing and couldn't see a way out. I would write down the way l felt and words of encouragement to myself, and it helped me heal. Writing became therapeutic for me and those words soon turned into this book.

Are you in a place of brokenness today? Give your pain to the Lord, only He has the ability to heal the deepest of wounds.

I made it, don't give up...........

GOD GAVE ME CLOSURE

A fter a breakup, disappointment or betrayal the first thing people always want to know is; "why?" Why did you hurt me? Why were you disloyal? Why did you betray me? Closure gives them a sense of peace that they were not the cause of the unpleasant that happened. It's always comforting to know that you are not the reason for something falling apart.

One morning, in a season where l was hurting the most, l went on my knees before God and wept like a baby. I told him l couldn't understand why bad things were happening to me and that l was so tired and drained from it all. How was it possible that someone could go through so much? Did He not care that l was hurting? Was He turning a blind eye to my pain? I was so broken and deeply wounded. As l knelt there sobbing, God began to show me things about myself l was unmindful of. He gave me the closure that l had been seeking all these years and that is "l was called for a purpose."

For that reason, it preordained that l couldn't just live the way l pleased or settle with any random person, regardless of the standard set by the world. I was set apart for purpose and destiny and that meant living a consecrated life. Fornication wouldn't work, shacking up wouldn't succeed, taking short cuts would never help me get ahead; because 1 was called for destiny. Now it all made sense why every other thing 1 had tried in the past just did not flourish. It gave me such an overwhelming sense of peace to know that God loved me that much to want better for me, even when 1 didn't think it was what 1 needed. He also unveiled to me that if certain things had worked out the way 1 had hoped in the past, 1 would have missed out on all the wonderful things he had predestined for me.

For years 1 had been going around seeking closure from people who couldn't care less that 1 was hurting, and in many instances; 1 would not find it. Get to a place where you stop asking those that hurt you for closure because in most cases, they never give it you. You pound and pound on them looking for answers, but to no avail. Seek your closure in God, He will reveal things to you that are hidden from the naked eye.

OUT OF MY GREATEST ADVERSITY CAME MY GREATEST REAKTHROUGH

———— ·•✦·• ————

In my worst affliction is where l was purified, refined and grew the most. You will think its torture until you see what is birthed out of it. Isn't it somewhat strange, that the things that broke you the most, end up helping you? Sometimes everything appearing to be going wrong, is you becoming all that God purposed you to be, it is a build up to your destiny. The things that hurt me taught me obedience, they drew me closer to God. Heartache, betrayal and despair taught me the importance of being submitted to God and that a life not built on Him, is in vain. What broke me birthed a book that will impact a great multitude of people, and leave a legacy of resilience. Betrayal set me up for greatness and because l wrote this book, for generations to come, many will not give up.

There is concealed power and an advantage in the things that often break us. I never knew what l carried until l was put in a situation where my power had to be revealed. The power that lay dormant in me, was suddenly awoken. Out of my greatest adversity came my greatest breakthrough but as it happened, it was unsparing and wearisome. Adversity forced open the giftings on my life, and it pushed me grow. It fueled me to do better not only for myself, but others too. Out of it came my utmost humility, growth and sincerity. God can turn your greatest grief, into your greatest comeback and testimony but first; you must give your pain to Him. Not another man or woman, drugs, weed or escapades; give your pain to the Master.

The only time adversity doesn't make way for what it's supposed to, is when the individual involved chooses to remain in the same cycle of things. They are passive about their pain and don't get tired of giving power to disruptive ways. Refuse to go through adversity and come out the same.

As baseless as it may sound you can soar above whatever you may be going through. I know this because there are many who have survived what you may be experiencing, and turned it into victory. Out of adversity has been a birth of authors, lawyers, millionaires, entrepreneurs, doctors, great women and men who dared to confront their odds. Out of my adversity was birthed an author and a book that will change the world. What you overcome, you do so for many others. Because of what you've survived, someone else just got a second chance at life.

Betrayal altered a lot in my life. As I've witnessed from my past experiences, betrayal stings because it is often riddled with lies, deceit and malice. It slanders your character so badly to a point where no one will want to associate with you. When somebody deliberately tarnishes your image, it is to validate themselves for the unjust things they did to you. Their regret needs consolation and the only way is to make you look as disgraceful as possible to everyone else. It gives them a sense of comfort that their double dealings, deception and what they did to you, was not as dreadful.

But as much as they can try to conceal and misrepresent the truth, what they meant for your humiliation and shame will turn into honor and nobility for you. Forgive them and release it from your heart. What they did was inexcusable but, this is where you gain repose and let God fight for you. Find peace in knowing that your vindication will come from the Lord.

The man who hurt me the most was conceited. On one occasion I asked him why he kept lying about me and his response was; "he will stop when I start behaving." He tarnished my image to a level that some no longer wanted to be in my circle because they now knew me as trouble. He wanted everyone else to resent me the way he did. One morning whilst praying, I poured out my heart to God about how much all this was deeply hurting me. I was worried about my reputation because this man had discredited and ruined me. As I knelt there weeping before God he gave me a specific chapter and verse to read that is Isaiah 17:13. At first, I was reluctant to open it because I thought maybe my mind was clouded with so many emotions, and I was imagining things. What if it wasn't even related to what I had just been praying about? I was in my healing season and still learning how to hear from God, so l was quite nervous when He directed me to a definite scripture. Nonetheless l opened it and it read:

"But though they thunder like breakers on a beach, God will silence them." (NLT)

In that moment l knew He was reassuring me that He would defend me in my absence and silence every tongue that rises against me. When God said no weapon formed against you will prosper, it included silencing every lying tongue. Your story will end in honor, dignity and vindication. First comes the shame, then comes the double honor, sometimes you have to take a bow to birth greatness.

Not every day will be the same, the reality is some days will be harder than others. Some moments you will feel so strong but others completely helpless. You will gasp and bleed but always know that; yes, it will scar you, but it will not kill you. Some days you will go to bed and wish to never wake up but it doesn't have to end in misery, devastation or hopelessness. Adversity should end in triumph.

I'm not sure if Joseph would have ever ruled Egypt had he not gone through all that he did. Its purpose when it not only delivers you, but a multitude. The whole of Egypt turned to God because of one man. His adversity was God setting him in place to impact a nation and generations. There is always a greater glory than your struggles. If it doesn't end in glory just know God is not done yet, it has to end in victory. It has to end with people wanting to know who this God in you is. Whatever unpleasant situation you may find yourself in, know that God has the ability to create a beautiful story, out your most unfortunate circumstances.

Don't give up!

---•◆❧◆•---

*You will tell your story someday, not to reopen old
wounds but to pour hope into and show somebody
else that; no matter the adversity there's a rainbow
on the other side of it all. Your scars serve as an
attestation to what you've survived. Scars are
beautiful when they can help somebody heal. That's
the beauty in scars.*

---•◆❧◆•---

I USED MY PAIN FOR GOOD

―――――・◦✵✿✵◦・―――――

Pain changes people; I've never seen anyone go through it, and remain the same. Some turn into hateful people because of the damage it did to them. They want others to feel what they felt, and it is in a sense comforting to them to know that they are not the only ones experiencing that hurt. They want everyone to hurt with them, and find contentment when others are as broken as they are. Don't be so comfortable with pain that you lose your human integrity. What you allow pain to change you into, becomes traits in your character. It begins to show in your choice of words and how you treat other people.

I know it may be difficult, but the ultimate goal for any human being should be to see others not go through what they did, because they know and understand the agony of being at your bottommost. Self-destructing and inflicting pain on others because you're hurt, will breed more damaged people. True healing comes when you use your pain to help somebody else heal, so l began to use my pain for good. I started to write down words of encouragement to myself and when I'd share that with other people, it resonated with them so much and they acknowledged how much it was helping them.

I found fulfillment in seeing others heal and become whole, so in principle; it's about what you do with your pain. Healing often comes when *62*
you take your own tragedies and the things that broke you, and use them as a means to help others. When they heal, you heal too. I never gave up so I could help another person, not to give in. Something in me changed greatly, it stopped being about me and became about us. Nobody was going to give up on my watch, no one was going to end their life if I could do something about it. So, I wrote a book, I told my story to encourage somebody not to throw in the towel because I too went through the storm, but made it out on the other side. That is how your vision should be set up, to pull up as many people with you as possible, it should not be self-serving.

Your story can only be told by you, don't let anybody rob you of your truth. It is you who felt the pain, it is you who experienced the trauma. It is you who bears the scars, and it is you who wept like a baby. It is you who survived it. Share it and release it because somebody will find hope, in your scars. You want to overcome? Use your pain for good.

Positive affirmation: "My heart will heal; my pain will serve me and others."

It is irrationality to think we can do life alone. Never take for granted the power and significance of prayer. Always acknowledge that there is a higher power ready to move in on your weakness. You can't receive help from a power you don't acknowledge first.

PART 3

PRAYER BECAME A FOUNDATIONAL PART OF MY LIFE

————••✦••————

People deal with adversity in different kinds of ways. I learned never to make that mistake of thinking that human beings or substances have all the answers. Not only is it unfounded, but impossible. In my adversity, I called on a higher power because I finally understood that there are certain things that only a supernatural being (God) can fix. If money was the solution, millionaires wouldn't be committing suicide. If drugs were the answer there would be no one dying from substance abuse. If cheap thrills were the means of solving it, then infidelity and recklessness would not be wrecking homes and ruining lives. None of these would be a cause for concern. It matters how you process every emotion because it determines who you will become on the other side of adversity. Will you come out refined or contaminated?

I chose to call upon the one who created the earth and put me in it, I didn't turn to alcohol, drugs, weed or adventures. I did not use another person as my remedy to get over heartbreak or life challenges, instead I asked God to heal my heart. He wove me, surely if there was somebody who knew me in depth, it was Him. He knew everything I would need to overcome adversity and it certainly wasn't what the world deems as the standard.

People often opt for an instant solution, they want to numb the pain but not deal with the root. They think about what they can binge to be freed from the pain, the shots they could take to forget. They think of who they can call to keep them company through their misery. All they want is to not feel anything in that particular moment. What they don't realize is; you may sweep the surface, but the root remains. When they keep going around in circles, they wonder why nothing seems to be changing or getting better. Indulgence, casual relations and weed are not solutions to anything and never will be. Those are temporary fixes, it is God who is an everlasting remedy. Humanity strives to fix the surface, but God works to remove the root so it never stems up again.

In God every answer can be found, His way is unsurpassed, incomparable and unmatched. Acknowledge His power and supremacy over everything because, there's only so much you can do in your own human strength. Prayer aligns and brings into order things that are concealed. He will give you the business ideas to get out of debt, He will put the right people on your path, He will make things available to you for a shift in your life. Everything should begin with Him because it is impossible for human beings to solve everything, you will always need a higher power.

Prayer gives you confidence to pull through, knowing that you are not alone. Even after prayer challenges may come to quiver you up, but you've got to have strong mental steadfastness that you won't be shaken. Know that after you've prayed in faith, God will do His part. Don't wonder or be impatient nor be troubled or anxious, the one that promised will deliver. When you have peace it's a symbol that you have faith that, what you prayed for will come to be.

Always begin with prayer, it is an unwavering foundation.

---◆✦◆---

Write down what you would like to see happen, then play it over and over again in your mind; it will keep your hope alive. When its blueprinted in your mind, manifestation reinforced by God becomes foreseeable. You can create a whole new life in your mind, by using the power of your imagination.

---◆✦◆---

I VISUALIZED

---•◦✦◦•---

One of the first steps to changing your life is visualization but, it should align with the purpose of God. To move from where you currently are you must first see where you're headed in the place of your mind. The achievements, the people, the places, the good health and success. Create a life in your mind that you want to see manifest, even the impossible.

If you are in a deep pit of despair and can't seem to find your way. Begin to think on things getting better and your life completely turning around, till you get to a point where the place you're in, can no longer shut you in. When your mind enlarges and you create the ideal life in it, you become too small for certain places. Don't give into feelings of discontentment and weariness, every situation is changeable; but first, you've got see it with the eye of your mind. Just because your expected ending has not materialized, does not mean your fate is sealed. You can love again, you can own a business and you can be debt free, hold on to that image of everything coming together. Its normal that you can get so tired, and your desires may seem so far out of reach but don't give in. Hold on to that mental picture, it will see you through. Even when nothing around you seems to be changing, keep that vision alive.

As you acquaint yourself with visualization, always strive for greatness and the extraordinary. Sometimes limitations are not only physical but in the mind. When I glare at the dreams I still desire to fulfill, I reason that maybe it's too much and how is it ever going to happen? I suppose when you look at your dreams and don't chuckle and slightly laugh at yourself; you just might be dreaming in limits. Your dreams should daze you too. Even if your reality may not currently be in sync with the ideal life you've built in your mind, just hold onto that mental image. Some people are ahead because they saw something that everybody else could not see. What do you see for yourself? Maybe you stumbled and lost focus along the way, but start to dream and believe in something again. Don't let life make you forget who you are, in such moments you have to realize that you can create new dreams. As you envision your future, strive to ensure that seasonal things don't become a lifetime norm. What you take on shouldn't be about survival or doing it to just get by, it should rather be about passion and making a difference in other people's lives. There is no limit to your dreaming because it happens in the realm of your mind, only you can confine yourself.

You've also got to believe in your dreams more than anybody else, so that you're not disheartened by people who think you can't do it. If you walked up to me and said you want to be the next Bill Gates, l would believe you. You know why? It's because, it is what you deem possible in your mind. If you are convinced of it, anybody else's opinion no longer matters. Nobody can stop you, but you. Don't be in your own way, don't let your mind be a stumbling block. In whatever it is you desire to become, see yourself as that. If you are janitor see yourself as owning your own cleaning services company. If you are an educator see yourself building schools. Maybe you are a doctor, imagine yourself opening your own practice. In sales as well, one can begin to envision themselves owning their own consultancy firm.

There will be moments where you may begin to blame the environment for stifling your growth, but as you look at other people who have managed to build and keep their integrity in that same scenery; let it challenge you to do better. A lot of things begin internally, and that is the way you think and perceive life. Where somebody else saw a tree, another saw books and papers. You've got to begin to see and think better.

You dream as far as the scope of your mind, constantly expose yourself to places and people that will challenge you to always see there is more. Ones that will awaken and enlarge your dreams. If you have the capacity to do so, travel the world as much you can because in some instances, dreams are triggered by what we see around us.

DARE TO DREAM, AND DON'T GIVE UP!

Your words have creative power let them be ones
that build, nurture and propel you to places beyond
your wildest imagination.
You speak because you understand that world was
created from a spoken word, "let there
be and it was so."

I SPOKE WHAT I WANTED TO SEE HAPPEN

—••❧••—

There were times my environment wasn't the picture of what I desired. I knew what God had promised but I just didn't know how to get through the now. What was I to do in my waiting for my heart's desires and His promises to manifest? God then made me understand that in waiting, is where you thank Him for the things you're trusting Him for. It's the place where you call and confess things that are not as though they were.

Romans 4:17 reads:
"God, who gives life to the dead and calls those things which do not exist as though they did."
(NKJV)

Even when you are in pain, you affirm that you are healed. When you are in need, you uphold that those needs are met. Never underestimate the power of audibly saying things out, that's how faith arises. You have to hear something, so let it be positive. Speak what you hope will happen.

These are some of the things I declared and affirmed to myself:

- I am a woman of real distinction
- I a woman of faith

- I am creative
- I am intelligent
- I am healthy and will flourish
- My heart will heal
- Things will get better
- I choose faith

I affirmed so much more, but this is to give you an idea of the element of building positive momentum in your life, through spoken words. When you have chosen faith, it will show in your vocalized words, you will keep confessing and affirming the positive whether you feel like it or not. Sometimes you have to say it out loud, your mind needs to hear it so that it is reinforced in your heart so much that it becomes a deeper inner conviction. "Yes, I'm hurting but my heart will heal, yes it's hard but things will get better, yes 1 lost the job but greater is coming, yes, I'm frustrated but God will make a way." Speak what you hope will happen, your words have creative power, eventually it shall be in existence.

There are days 1 would literally place my hand over my heart and say, *my heart will heal, things will get better.* I would say within myself, *"what 1 may be feeling is unbearable, it feels like death sometimes but 1 choose faith; 1 choose hope."*

There will be moments where doubt can try to creep in, but persistently keep confessing and wait patiently for manifestation. What you say within and aloud matters in your season of waiting. Without realizing it we sometimes cloud our minds with negative thoughts, because of down cast spoken words. Things such as "it's taking too long, everybody around me seems to be making it, maybe all this is just not for me." You have the rule to direct your thoughts, why not shift them to *"yes l will excel, God is making a way, my health shall be restored, all that is good and perfect is mine."*

What you hear goes through your ear, it is then retained in your mind then lodged deeply in your heart. That's where you should hide the positive. So, as long as it won't build or add to your change, do not let it out of your mouth. Speak what it true not factual, speak into existence the change you want to see, come to be. You get through the now by leaning on the word of God and declaring the things you hope for and desire. Even when you feel the pain keep proclaiming healing, when you see the chaos keep speaking peace, when you see the debt speak provision. Become so stubborn in faith that even when you see things still not changing, or to all appearances seem to be getting worse; continue affirming the changes. Your words are seeds, they will come to fruition.

I used to be such a one, who watched others go ahead of me. I would watch them receive their miracles and breakthroughs, and wonder when my turn is coming. I would feel so left behind and it was as though good things were happening to everyone else, but me. But as I stood in faith and continued to speak the things I desired to come into fullness in my life; God blew my mind. Sometimes when you are in waiting and anticipating God to do the most in your life, it may take a while but when it finally comes through; He will show out for you. Do your part then wait on Him patiently in faith.

Don't give up, speak it into existence.

---·◆~---

Your faith is your greatest weapon.
It is what keeps your hope alive in moments of
despair. Though it may not be logical to believe in
something you do not see yet, it
ignites feelings of expectation for manifestation. So,
you just believe because faith is that which
keeps you from losing heart.
With a muffled voice and tears in your eyes; you just
believe.

---·◆~---

I WALKED BY FAITH

Faith is a fight.

There are circumstances in life that will require nothing but your faith, there will be situations that sheer human strength cannot fix. In those moments, there won't be a single person with the capacity to help but God, and it somewhat leaves you with not much of a choice, but to stir up your faith.

Nothing teaches faith like dry seasons. I learned to walk by faith in the midst of adversity. Faith is purposely disregarding the now because you perceive the conclusion will be glorious. It is not being ignorant, but rather shifting your focus onto the greater end than what may not be working in the now. It is feeling the pain of sickness, heartbreak, lack or debt but still choosing to give it no mind and decree, "l can be healed, l will not lack and l shall be free." The whole world was created by the unseen. Faith feels like being blindfolded and letting God take a hold of your hand, and lead you through a place you can't see. Though you may not see where you are going, but you trust that He who holds your hand won't let your foot slip or graze a stone.

Before this book was set to be released l had an intense battle that l was fighting. I would pray and ensured that l did what was obligatory of me, but it didn't seem to be changing the way 1 hoped it would. It made me understand that the enemy would rather destroy you now than let you get to your destiny, he really is afraid that you'll change the world. It's a threat to him when you come to the fullness of who you were created to be. What will happen when you become a "godly" world renowned author, lawyer, doctor or business mogul? Anything done in a truthful way is animosity with him. So, he begins to send distractions in the form of trials on your path, he uses silent weapons in the form of unruly thoughts, frustration, depression and worry but don't be shaken by them or what you currently see.

What then one needs to do is reposition, recharge and not slack because there is a lot riding on what you do in the now. Use every weapon within your reach but above all, use your greatest one; that is faith. It is by it that you will you will be able to quench all the flaming arrows of the enemy as accorded in Ephesians 6:16:

"In all circumstances take up the shield of faith, with which you can extinguish all the faming arrows of the enemy."

I began to apply that word in my life, when nothing around me seemed to be getting better. I held onto that mental picture of things changing for good. I would whisper within, "I'm heavy hearted but 1 choose faith, I'm devastated but 1 choose faith, I'm nervous but 1 choose faith, I don't understand but 1 still choose faith." I stirred up my faith strongly; I had to win.

I refused to be intimidated or back down, I grew stubborn in a good way. Some moments will be so agonizing and you will feel as though you can't go on, but gain power over those feelings of hopelessness because it is by faith that you will overcome. Pass that test of trusting God, don't let your faith fail.

I'm impelled by the story of Sarah in the book of Genesis. Imagine that you are a ninety-year-old woman, and God is making it known to you that you will bear your first child? It sounds ridiculous and biologically impossible, even Sarah laughed to herself because she could not see how it was even conceivable. God then asked her husband Abraham why she laughed? I think He asked the question in disbelief that somebody He created questioned His abilities? I picture God looking down from heaven thinking "does she even know who I am?" He went on to ask Abraham if there was anything too hard for Him?

This is what happens in our own lives at times. We read of God's promises and rationalize, but can He really do this? Oh yes, He can; yes, He can! God will always fight for you but he needs you to meet Him at the point of faith. If I did not have faith this book would not have been published. The enemy knew that it would get to people about to throw in the towel, some about to take their own lives. My book is a threat to his kingdom but I stood my ground, refused to be intimidated and held on strong in faith. I kept confessing the word and trusted that my life will unfold in a desirable way because I understood that the purpose of God, cannot be stopped.

Walk by faith, have firm trust and belief that what you desire can happen. Proverbs 23 vs 18 says:

"For surely there is a hereafter, and your hope will not be cut off."
NKJV)

The coming of your desires is dependent on your faith. You receive what you have faith for. No matter how impossible it may seem, if you believe it is so, it shall be yours. Don't reason it out too much, just trust the one who promised. When the eye is on the prize, the cramping in your leg won't stop you, the negative voices won't deter you because you are rushing to grab what you've seen with the eye of your mind. Faith has shown you what is true and you just have to get a hold of it.

Along the way your faith will be challenged greatly, but what will keep you from losing heart; is belief. In my journey I held on because I believed I would see my breakthrough, healing, wealth and vindication, so I did not lose heart. Understand that it is not that God can't do it for you, the question is; do you have faith for it? Every victory or success story has an element of faith, they had to believe in something. Your faith is your greatest advantage, don't allow your mind to be in the way of your miracle. In my walk I became adamant that 1 would never stop believing and trusting God. Yes, my faith will be tested, but 1 was so firm in that it will be my trademark. Ask a mother who is at the bedside of a terminally ill child. She is at a place where she fully comprehends that this is beyond the doctor, or any other human being and that the only choice left, is to just have faith that God will work a miracle. So, she begins to raise her faith for the miraculous and watches God do the impossible.

Dare to trust the One who has no limits. What is it you are hoping for, let your faith run into your miracle.

---·◆❧◆·---

*Purity is a woman's covering. It will preserve
and safeguard her heart. Your body is a
consecrated place, a sanctuary not to be
dishonored. The only to access it , is the man
who has made a commitment; and one you
confirmable call your husband.*

---·◆❧◆·---

I WALKED IN PURITY

Purity will preserve you...

I know in the society we live in it is considered laughable and shunned upon but, it safe guards no one, but you. Giving honor to your body serves you. Purity will preserve you from anything that threatens to corrupt your serenity. One of the things that pressed strongly on my heart in my journey is that God is a holy God, and outside of holiness, l was far from His will. So, l purposed to live a consecrated life.

To try and divulge on this subject of purity l thought of approaching it from the perspective of a question l have heard countless times and that is; "why do people cheat." Amongst other excuses I've been privy to and seem most common are recklessness, lack of discipline, cheap thrills, lustful desires, entitlement, loneliness and curiosity. In my inquest to try and fully understand this whole controversy that has the whole world buzzing, I began to do my own fact finding and there's one particular thing l came across that gave me a rude awakening and that is; "SOUL TIES."

So, what has that got to do with cheating? The truth is; sex was created for the confines of marriage only, but it has since been desecrated and turned into a random and erratic thing. People do so without realizing that whether they treat it as something without emotional intimacy or commitment, it does not take away the spiritual repercussions. Just because you may not immediately see the effects with the naked eye, does not mean you've gotten away with it. Many have the impression that as long as they don't commit, they've got nothing to worry about.

The reality is; there is an unintended consequence that comes with casual sex, and it's called a "soul tie". If not dealt with it is then taken into marriage or your next relationships and in most cases culminates to infidelity.

For example, a man or woman can wake up with a wave of emotions of missing their previous partner. Where are all those emotions coming from; "SOUL TIES." Because there's a part of you that's still carrying around a part of them, it may indicate that there is an unhealthy emotional connection. When you have sex with somebody, in the spiritual realm there's a unification that occurs. You take on what they are and in turn they take on who you are.

Whether you move on in the physical, you can retain parts of them without even being cognizant of it. That is why when confronted on their actions some people say, "it just happened." It didn't just happen, the connection to whom they were with in the past, is still existent inside of them and once in a while it is triggered. So, the first opportunity they get to reach out, their instinct is to pick up the phone and call that person. Your picking up the phone is an emotional response to what you carry. You begin to long and desire to see them again overlooking the fact that it will compromise what you currently have. The emotions are so strong such that they cloud your reasoning and sense, and you become oblivious to the consequences. Though it is true that people can be reckless with strangers, it is more prevalent with people that they have history with; hence my above example.

If you begin to look at a human being as somebody with a spirit, soul and body, your eyes will be opened to the understanding that, certain actions don't just have effects on the body alone but the spirit too and you will tread with vigilance. To show that soul ties are real, take a moment to notice how you begin to take on the mannerisms, facial expressions, wording of the people you have relations with without even noticing. Those little gestures or body language; you find yourself unconsciously mimicking who they are. Puzzled you wonder, "when did 1 start speaking that way or using those gestures?" That is the strength of soul ties.

After that inquisition 1 concluded that the same way the body needs a regular detox, so does the spirit. Soul ties to be broken and unhealthy things to be prayed away lest they be left lingering and spring up along away.

Out of all the sins God said sexual sin was different from the rest because; you sin against your own body. 1st Corinthians 6:18 asserts that:

"There is a sense in which sexual sins are different from all others. In sexual sin we violate the sacredness of our bodies." (MSGE)

Sexual sin is the easiest entrance for the enemy to attack and ensnare you. It gives him a foothold over your life. When he has roped you in that lifestyle he stifles your liberation to make sure you never reach your destiny.1st Corinthians 6:16 further says:

"There's more to sex than mere skin on skin. Sex is as much a spiritual mystery as physical fact, the two become one." (MSGE)

How many people are you willing to become one with, before finally getting to the right person? How much spiritual baggage do you want to keep dragging along with you? God desires that we give honor to our bodies and treat them like sanctuaries. For many the challenge is they are trying to escape or compensate for something that is not right in their lives. You've got to deal with the root of the issue because it is unhealthy to be dependent on sex, drugs or anything other than God for balance, happiness and emotional highs. There is something seriously amiss if you cannot function without things that are detrimental to your spirit and health.

Apart from the word of God, it is hard to honor Him because that is the benchmark to living a pure life as conferred in Psalms 119:9:

"How can a young person stay pure? By obeying your word." (NLT)

The challenge is the world views sex as an act of the body alone. The actuality is, a human being is spirit, body and soul. When you sleep with multiple people it doesn't only affect your body, but your spirit too. Quoting the message bible,1st Corinthians 6:12 reads:

"Just because something is technically legal, doesn't mean that its spiritually appropriate."

Some things may look good, but may not be necessarily beneficial. Don't lose yourself in an effort to stay cool and relevant. Sex within matrimony is your covering and honor, but outside those confines; it uncovers you and brings about shame. This is not to say there is no redemption, when you heart is truly repentant you can come to a place of full restoration. Begin to walk in purity and honor the sacredness of your body.

———··◆⟡◆··———

Obedience will cost you something. It could be a relationship, friendship, habits, pleasures, cheap thrills or a certain lifestyle. The ultimatum is God or that thing? And as fate would have it, no one has ever won by choosing the latter. Dealing with the discomfort of discipline, is better than dealing with the grief of disobedience....

———··◆⟡◆··———

PART 4

I WALKED IN OBEDIENCE

———••❖❦❖••———

L et your will be done" is the most difficult, yet most sincere and life changing prayer one could ever say. Obedience is what will line you up with purpose. There are certain things that will not manifest, until you're in a place of submission to God. Personally, my journey has been filled with so many experiences and encounters with different people that led me to understand the power of obedience, and the favor that comes with it. In one occurrence somebody said to me, "the giftings on your life are great but for them to be made manifest, you need to position yourself and submit to the will of God for your life."

At the time 1 couldn't quite understand what those gifts were, and what it meant to walk in obedience. I had no knowledge or understanding on writing a book and 1 did not quite have a vision for my life. But as 1 matured, it began to make sense. When 1 truly submitted to God, He began to show me who 1 was and the hidden abilities 1 carried. The things that broke me brought me to a place of total surrender to Him. Often those experiences that agonize us, teach us obedience. They bring us to our knees such that our posture becomes that of submission to God.

Obedience is uncomfortable, the thought of saying goodbye to things that gave you fulfillment but were damaging to your spirit and soul, is not a simple thing to do. It will mean forfeiting a few things but for your long-term benefit. It will mean no more living the way you want and see right in your own eyes but instead, what truly is the resolve of God. The challenge is we want the best of both worlds, we are bent on living the way we see fit, but still desire the hand of God to be upon it. God wouldn't ask you to release something unless He knew it was unfavorable to your well-being and would burn you in the end. I had to let go off toxic relationships because they were one of my biggest downfalls.

There is nothing that should be able to bargain with your soul. Things that do so are ones you are willing to compromise for; be it a relationship, fame or money. By not listening to the voice of God you are doing yourself an injustice because all He wants, is the best for you.

Each time 1 went against the will of God, 1 found myself in places of deep despair that only He could get me out of. God can speak to you about your destiny whilst in your sin, but manifestation occurs in a place of obedience. Until 1 wholly submitted to God, 1 stayed stuck in certain places longer than intended. In disobedience you delay purpose and destiny.

Understand that your obedience will affect a whole lineage, never take that for granted. When you get it right you do so for many generations to come.

Romans 5:19 declares:

"Because one person disobeyed God, many became sinners. But because one other person obeyed God, many will become righteous."
(NLT)

Disobedience can cost you severely, 1 know you want the temporary fulfillment, maybe everyone is conforming or maybe you feel left out but the moment you crumble, the consequences are harsh. The will of God is good, but from afar it looks nothing like it till you finally get to walk in it. People tend to wait for a near death experience or an unfortunate incident for them to finally submit to God. God desires to start on a clean slate with you. He doesn't want you to push Him aside, just to reach what you desire. But He doesn't come uninvited or impose himself on people, you have to invite Him into your heart. When 1 devoted myself to walking in the will of God, I stood firm on not going back to the things that tore me from Him. I stood resolute in that, I wasn't going back to the things that broke me or dysfunction.

Many might say, "but 1 have tried everything and it just doesn't seem to be working." Have you tried walking in obedience? There may be certain clarifications as to why things may be the way they are in your life. In unique instances some may be victims but, be careful that you're not in a place of anguish because of the circumstances you shaped. When you're in the will of God you are travailing for righteousness, when you're outside the will of God you are suffering for sin. Take a moment to reflect on your life, to see which may be true.

There were times l wasn't so smart, made bad decisions and blamed God for it. But when l truly began to put Him first with the most sincere and obedient heart, l watched him blow my mind. I marvel at the life l almost lost out on because of disobedience. Who and what could you possibly be, if you made better choices and chose obedience? What are you willing to change, to live life to the uttermost?

God redeems us even in our mistakes and bad choices, it's about the position of your repentant heart. Choose obedience today.

I BROKE OUT OF STAGNATION

There comes a time in life that individuals should sit down and re-evaluate their lives. Until you've reached breaking point you will never get up and do something different. A strong desire for change will show in your elevated commitment to reading the word of God, books, prayer, researching, or any positive thing that will help you break out of where you currently are.

When this year began 1 wanted to see a change that I had never experienced before in my entire life. There was such a desperation in my heart for better so, when others were blowing up fire crackers and celebrating the crossover to the new year, 1 was on my knees pleading with God to change my life and do something in me that nobody had ever seen. Because of those sacrifices I've truly seen His hand at work in my life.

You have to refuse to settle in calamitous conditions and come to a resolution that you want better for yourself. A better career, health, finances and relationships. Personally, 1 began to feel uncomfortable with stagnation and became unsettled about certain things in my life. Surely there had to be better. I wasn't content with a struggling career, sickness, lack or anything distressing. Always remember that you have the control to see better for yourself. There are people building in the emptiest of places, not because its necessarily a conducive environment, but because something in them sees more and better for themselves. You have a part to play in your liberation by believing that your life can be better.

I recall a time in my life when l would have constant dreams of seeing myself in a car and each time l would try to accelerate, it just wouldn't move. Strangely l would end up forcefully using my legs to shift the car, almost as if l was carrying its weight. In other instances, l would be in an exam room struggling to finish a high school examination and wake up in so much panic. It made me anxious because in reality, l had completed those exams; so what was the meaning of that dream?

I try not to obsess much over dreams but l do take note of them and over time l gained understanding of what they possibly meant. When l looked at my life it made sense why l was going around in circles, l would have short lived success and then major downfalls, I just seemed to be stuck in one place. Those dreams in a sense symbolized stagnation.

So, l began to pray strongly about my career and asked God to show me the direction l was to take. It was so sincere and l truly believed He would give me an answer. It so happened that l started to have certain encounters with different people that served as a confirmation that my career would be propelled. But, I now had to figure out the what, how and when?

What was I going to do, how and when was it going to happen? I spent the next couple of months trying to figure things out till the day I started writing. I woke up one morning and just started writing. In my mind I was simply pouring out my heart and thoughts. Little did I know I would one day stand as an author. I got so many confirmations from people I shared my pieces with. They found hope and healing from my words, and so they encouraged me to keep writing; and I did.

Breakout of stagnation in prayer and in your mind too. Why prayer first? Because it straighten outs the hidden with the physical through a higher power; that is God. Sometimes stagnation is a result of undiscovered purpose and abilities. The day I discovered my purpose I broke out of stagnation. Self-discovery is critical, and the first point of contact is God.

After you have prayed, you then build your mental capacity. Get your mentality out of the, "I'm too old for this" and that only good things happen to other people but you. Snap out of that reasoning, all those negative elements you reason out in your mind should not be given power.

I am very passionate about subduing the mind because you can read the most powerful books, attend life changing seminars on success, you can be in the presence of greatness or in the atmosphere of power, but gain nothing out of it if your mind is in a trapped state. Decades ago there were people who encountered the most powerful man (Jesus) when he was on earth, but profited nothing from it. There was nothing erroneous with him, neither was he incapable, the challenge was, the people were flawed in their thinking and faith. When you are tired of being the way you are, you begin to take God at his word because you truly want your life to change.

Many a time when we've fought something for so long, we become comfortable with it. It becomes our new normal and instead of trying to continue to change it, we simple build a life around it. In a season of adversity, it is very easy to become content with something that's not ideal. You become so familiar with pain, being down and out, not having enough to get by, failure, depression, sickness and being in chains. You then strive to build comfort around those dire circumstances, keep them under control, and just learn to live with it. Let that not be what you settle for.

In many situations you are defeated internally before you are externally. Defeat begins in your mind when you start thinking and whispering to yourself that, "this is the end, there's no way out, what life can one possibly have after this?" Everything else succumbs and you begin to do life overcome, it soon becomes a routine. You should never stop fighting until you've won. Sometimes results are not instant, you keep believing and affirming till it is manifested. Though it may take a while, know that life can get better.

With prayer, faith and a renewed mind, you too can break out of stagnation in your life.

Positive affirmation: Say out audibly; "I am breaking out of stagnation."

I READ BOOKS

———— ··◆♪♫◆·· ————

I can't even begin to describe what reading books did for me, it's almost as if a veil was lifted off my face and I started to see life in a whole different light. It dispelled things that clouded my mind, and the way I looked at adversity changed. The way I perceived wealth, love and success completely reformed. I started to dream big and challenge myself. As an aspiring author at the time I started to truly believe that I could be a great writer, even a best-selling author.

I began to dream the impossible……..

I did not start reading books knowing I was going to be an author in the imminent future. I read them because I saw how it transformed people's lives and I desired that for myself too. I got tired of being stagnant and financially ensnared, I had been going around in circles for such a long time and it was time to break out. There is so much power in reading and I have found so many answers hidden in a book.

There is one particular book by Dr Joseph Murphy, "The power of your subconscious mind" that completely challenged my intellect like never before. In his book he writes about learning the discipline of not finishing a negative sentence in your mind. I also took time to listen to his recordings on YouTube where he spoke specifically about wealth. He held the notion that if a negative thought about finances comes fifty times in one hour, reverse it each time by thinking and affirming; "God is my instant supply meeting every need." Since then my mental wealth has never been the same.

In my reading many other books, I grew in wisdom. When you read you discover truths you may have not known. I learned that the mind can be trained and mastered to what you desire your life to be. When you read, the scope of your mind is enlarged and challenges you to rethink your vision and goals. If they were too small you find yourself aspiring for greater. You might not be where you want to be, but there's something about reading that will get you where you desire to be.

As I habituated myself to reading, I became proactive. It challenged me to act on my dreams by fact finding what it takes to achieve them. As a would-be author I learned how to be more articulate with my words, I educated myself on what it takes to be a published, down to the correct font to use when writing, proof reading, editing and all the progressions invested in it. I had to acquire more knowledge about what I intended to achieve.

Reading will challenge and add on to your brainpower, it will force you to grow and reason better. It is one of the greatest investments to your mind. If you were never a reader challenge yourself to do so, even if its one book per month and as you accustom yourself to reading, growth is certain.

I never gave up because l read books, are you reading?

Just because you feel fear, it does not make you a weakling. Being courageous is choosing to ignore the things that frighten you most and charging forward knowing that; warriors are birthed on the battlefield. Take on those challenges, go out on a limb and believe that you have the ability to achieve what others deem impossible.

Don't be afraid to be the first of something, those who ever broke world records or invented the spectacular felt the fear, but chose to go against their feelings.

I DEALT WITH MY FEAR

———— ··◆⁂◆·· ————

There will be flashes when you will get small voices at the back of your mind whispering, what if it fails? "What if I never make it out of the valley? What if I never break free from what's binding me? What if I never get out of debt? What if I never excel in life?" If you can master the discipline of shutting down certain thoughts, you've mastered the art of victory.

In my journey I finally dealt with my fear. I overcame it to such a heightened level that, if I made a million dollars today and woke up with a zero-balance tomorrow, I wouldn't fret because I know and understand the power of Him who carries my life. There are certain things that won't phase you when you know you've got the creator of the earth backing you up. You face life with so much bravery and expectancy that as long as you have the greatest on your side nothing will intimidate you.

As I was writing this book I had a moment where I felt; maybe I'm being too ambitious, who am I to write a book? I felt so nervous and thought; perhaps I didn't think things through and I was in over my head. I was a woman in self-doubt and fear. What made me stand is the strong conviction in my heart that somebody out there needs my book. What is it that is making you fearful today, what is that thing you need to confront? Gain so much self-confidence that you begin to see no opportunity as out of your league.

There is a fear of failure that many possess, especially where wealth is concerned. Trusting in God means you know that even if the economy doesn't perform well you're taken care of. Stop fearing failure and being without for your day to day living. You are less fearful when you know who your trust is in. If it's in men you will be anxious, but if it's in God you have so much confidence that even if you could wake up with nothing, you know that He will take care of you. If the economy could crumble and you lost your businesses, property and cars you have assurance that God will restore it all.

Be it fear of losing money, failure, being hurt again or fear of the unknown, begin to confront those feelings because if left unchecked, they turn into a heap of unprocessed emotions and when left to linger, they become a hindrance to your development. To do life fearful is to do it confined. You are limited and crippled because every step you take is huddled with fear. Become a daring person and watch your life transform.

I know at times it's not that you don't believe that things can get better, it is fear and the strain of processing and living through your emotions when nothing is going right. But it is necessary to learn how to develop courage and handle issues confidently. Whatever it is that you are trying to break out of or pursue, let your peace be in knowing that, if it doesn't necessarily go the way you anticipated the first time, it is not the end. As I grew that is the attitude 1 adopted, I would whisper to myself that; "I will learn and do better." In moments when you seemingly can't convince your heart that everything will be alright, at least convince your mind, your feelings will catch up.

Developed courage comes with increased confidence. There was a time 1 would walk into a room and envisage that, 1 am the least. In my mind 1 would say things like, "what if people don't like me? What if they look down on me?" But as 1 matured 1 began to understand that without realizing, I'm feeding myself with the negative and it clogs my confidence and gives out that ambiance. So, 1 reformed my thoughts to, "people will love me, 1 am exceptional, 1 have great presence, there is a peace about me." I started to truly believe in myself. Confront you fears and insecurities and begin to walk in the boldness that God is for you. The first line of Deuteronomy 31:6 reads:

"Be strong and courageous."

You've got to believe that no matter what circumstance you may find yourself in, things can get better. *"It may seem unbelievable but keep saying within yourself, it will get better, 1 can attract better, 1 can possess greater and 1 can be better."* When the ground gets shaky and threatens to throw you flat on your face, find firm footing, wear courage on your shoulders and keep it moving. What's inside of you is far stronger than the rickety ground beneath you.

Positive affirmation: Say out audibly; "I will not walk in fear, I will be bold, courageous and confident."

*When it comes to reliability never have confidence in
anyone more than you do God, no matter how
powerful or influential you think they are. Have firm
belief in God's abilities and strength, for He is
consistent and never changes. Human beings have
flaws and can
  disappoint, sometimes not intentionally but it does
ensue. Let your heart be rooted in the right place,
trust God with your life because
what He offers comes with a guarantee, His words
never fall to the ground. He is not indecisive or
toyed around by mood swings, He always delivers.*

I PUT MY TRUST IN GOD NOT MaN

———— ••❀•• ————

In my season of growth l was reminded of an experience l had in high school that taught me the importance of leaning on God for everything pertaining to my life. In the year 2003 l walked into my final 'O' Level mathematics exam without a calculator in hand. Oddly the day before the exam, l did have one belonging to a friend of which we had agreed l would use it because she too would be using someone else's calculator. Last minute things shifted and she took hers back citing reasons that, the one she was hoping to use, was also demanded back by the owner.

By then l was already panicking because l had no plan B. When you are in a missionary boarding school, a stationery shop is not something that's in close proximity, so there is no way l could have improvised. I went to the lower level students in search of a calculator but most of them claimed they had already borrowed theirs to other students who were also writing their finals. I'm sure others had one to spare but felt uncomfortable with sharing their possessions.

I was devastated and cried myself to sleep that night. You must understand that this was my future, not some mid-term exam l could easily make up for. Our school was doing the calculator version of Mathematics so we were never taught how to use tables when it came to calculating all those complicated mathematical formulas. I had no idea how I would get through that section of the exam. The following morning I woke up in my grief and headed to the exam room. Without a calculator I had to use my fingers and written figures to analyze the simpler sums, but when it came to formulas I got stuck and those questions carried a lot of marks. I would work out questions to the level which did not require a calculator then leave it blank for the complicated calculations. I cried through the whole exam, it felt like a nightmare turned to reality. I just couldn't process how much I had lost out on. Out of a question that possibly carried eight marks, I probably scored three, the rest I lost.

I would only learn of my fate months later. When the results came out I had scored a C. I was grateful that I had passed but for such a longtime I was unsatisfied. I wondered what symbol I would have gotten, all things being equal. Could I have possibly missed out on an A or B? I felt so robbed, it just wasn't fair. I missed out on a better grade because of familiarity and over-reliance. This may have happened years ago, but the lesson I took away from that experience is the importance of preparation and having the wisdom of not putting too much confidence in human abilities. Right in your moment to shine and progress, those you had developed a dependence on, can pull out. It may be true that not everyone will disappoint you but it is wise to always fall back on a supernatural being (GOD). Let him always be the one backing you up and sustaining you. Don't put so much trust in men to be the ones to open doors for you, help you set up your business, meet your needs and give you opportunities because at some point they may fail you.

Psalms 118:8 states:

"It is better to trust in the Lord than to depend on people." (GNT)

Let God always be the provenance of your everything. Trust God to a point where if you ever lost everything and ended up on the streets, you are confident He will take care of you and restore you to your former glory. Nobody can ever be as consistent and dependable as He is. He never says something He does not mean. Your peace, joy, confidence, strength, comfort and finances should emanate from a superior being. Other sources can be cut off or run dry. Draw from a place that keeps promises and doesn't deliver based on feelings. A well that is beyond scientific understanding and defies the laws of nature.

I've gotten some NO's in my life and it taught me that l should never depend on anyone to make things work in my life. Trusting in God gave me so much peace and confidence and got rid of fear. l rested, I stopped worrying or being anxious because l finally understood the power of Him l had put my trust in. I felt so strong that l wouldn't crumble if l were faced with greater challenges because l developed great confidence in God. He is my covering whether l happen to be on the streets, just lost a house or a job, l know He will provide for me. Knowing the name of the Lord is what will set you on high, not your connections or who's high profile name you know. When you are His, you eat from His pasture because eating from the table of man comes in limited supply. But from His; sustenance is forever available.

From this moment begin to put your trust in the one who put you on this earth. You've got to be fully convinced of His power for it to work in your life. Put your trust in God.

———• ✦ ❧❧ ✦ •———

Forgive yourself first...........
Forgive yourself for the things you allowed to happen
when you didn't know better, weren't smarter or
wiser. Forgive the bad deci-
sions, failures, mistakes, betrayals, setbacks and
anything that held
you back. Self-condemnation can turn into a mental
prison of wallowing in pity and resentment towards
yourself. Only when you've forgiven yourself can you
truly forgive the other person because, you've first
made peace with you.

———• ✦ ❧❧ ✦ •———

PART 5

I FORGAVE MYSELF

———•◦✦◦•———

Have you ever had those moments where you just want to punch yourself in the face? Where you ask yourself how could l be so senseless? How could l be so naïve and gullible? In the past l cannot recall how many times l repeated over and over in my mind that l begrudged myself because of my failures and some of the choices and mistakes l had made in the past. I had begun to develop unkind feelings towards myself from the thoughts that l was breeding and playing over in your mind. l resented myself for the things that had happened to me. The issue was I would always seem to forgive everyone but myself, and everything that happened would haunt me when l was alone.

Self-condemnation can hit hard emotionally because you begin to question your lack of common sense and intelligence as to why you allowed certain things to happen. You could have been smarter and made better choices. It's unfortunate that the past cannot be changed, but it does not mean the future is fated either. Learn from your pit falls and vow to make better choices and decisions going forward. Forgive yourself for those things that, had you been mentally and emotionally matured; would have never happened. And when you've done so extend it to the other person, it will liberate you. Forgiveness is for your unshackling from bitterness, rage, anger or any ill feeling from unkind experiences.

You stumbled but did not fall, the stone may have grazed your toe and left you bleeding but walk on that limp till you find your stride. You now know to watch your step and be vigilant so you don't trip again. You've learned your lesson, forgive yourself and begin to do better.

There are also moments where you can cause pain to others without realizing it, forgive yourself for the times you weren't the one wronged. After you've forgiven yourself, give what's left over to God. He can use your wreckage and rough fragments to build a new life that looks nothing like your past. Give Him your pieces.

Positive affirmation: Say out audibly; "I forgive myself."

---·◆✦◆·---

Revenge is choosing instant gratification over lifelong peace. Entrust God with your injustices, true vindication and justice comes from Him. He is the master silencer of any tongue that rises against you.

---·◆✦◆·---

I GAVE MY INJUSTICES TO GOD

—————— ••✦✥✦•• ——————

Many a time the only thing on our minds after we are hurt is, "how can I get revenge?" We want those who hurt us to feel the intensity of the pain they caused us. We want the knife they lodged deep in our hearts to pierce theirs. It is hard to get even with those who did you wrong without pulling yourself down with them. Not only do you taint your image, but it is often accompanied with feelings of regret when everything flares up.

That is why vengeance is best left in the hands of a superior being. I know its hard-hitting but you have to give God his place when it comes to your injustices. Whether you are hurt in business, in a relationship, by friends or family release that anger and distress into His hands because, there is way He takes care of things, without tainting Himself. He remains pure and Holy even after settling the score. God will not overlook anything or forget everything you went through. Trust him with your pain. Release your anger, if it keeps a hold on you it will push you to do regretful things or sin. Psalms 37: 8 denotes that:

> *"Cease from anger and forsake wrath. Do not fret it only causes harm." (NKJV)*

Hebrews 10: 30 also says:
"Vengeance is mine, and l won't overlook a thing."
(MSGE)

God sees every unfair thing that happened to you. He saw those who laughed in the face of your pain, betrayal and capitalized on it. You will be misunderstood at times but rest in knowing that, all those who did not believe your truth, will see your vindication and justice. Don't harbor things that defile you, let go of your bitterness and rage because it does not hurt the person who caused it, but rather the one who carries it. You're hurting whilst they are living, unfair l know but don't do yourself a disfavor by holding onto dreadful emotions. God is asking you to release it all so you can have peace. Forgiveness is for your peace. When you are disgruntled or have feelings of bitterness towards those who hurt you, it takes nothing away from them but you. What and who do you need to forgive today?

Positive affirmation: Say out audibly; "l release every hurt and those responsible for it into your hands Lord."

*You cannot give to others what you first haven't
given to yourself.*

*You cannot receive from others what is authentic if
you do not know what it feels or looks like. Give
yourself love, give yourself
care and grace so that when you do love, you do so
from your overflow, not what you have left. When
you've poured into you, nobody can approach you
with inadequacies. Be so familiar with love that
you know and discern when you are being
shortchanged. You must be given the regard you
deserve; but it begins with you.*

I LEARNED TO LOVE MYSELF

————••❦••————

When 1 truly embraced my worth, nobody could shortchange me anymore. It wasn't out of arrogance, but gained confidence that 1 too am deserving of what's respectable. I had to make sure there was an infilling of so much love in me first, so that 1 could set the standard of what people should be giving to me when they walk into my life. When you have first given love to yourself, you will be able to clearly discern when someone is depriving you of what is rightful. If you truly love yourself there are certain things you won't allow. The things 1 so desired to give to others 1 had to make sure they are poured into me first so that when authentic love comes, I would love from my overflow. Often when we think of the idea of love, it is that we give it to others first and neglect ourselves. When you've loved yourself, you can now truly love another at the level you do yourself.

After my greatest hurt that almost consumed me 1 purposed that 1 would never settle for anything less than 1 truly deserved. I was at peace about not being married for the rest of life if 1 never found authentic love. I didn't want to marry for pain or for, "that's all there is so take it." I didn't want to marry to be broken, I wanted to marry for peace, purpose and destiny. The leftovers that the world was serving were not worth it. The bare minimum wasn't worth it, the, "at least I've got something" wasn't worth it. The, "it's better than nothing" just wasn't worth it. I desired what was real. If it wasn't like Christ loved the church l didn't want it.

In the past l had never known what it truly meant to be loved, to be fought hard for, to have someone put you first before themselves apart for God. Outside of Him, l was naive as to what love is. The earthly one l had experienced burned, it wounded deeply and made you sink into depression. It weighed you down, filled you with rage, made you bitter and weep. It broke your spirit and made your soul weak. It left you torn, shattered, exposed and ashamed. It whispered; "you're nothing, you're worthless." Surely that couldn't have been love. I wanted to be the miracle of love in a world where people say faithfulness is a myth. To be a good example in this generation that it was possible to be faithful through marriage, be disciplined and to say no to temptation. In that season of learning to love myself, l also learned what it meant to be selfless. I had to make sure l was becoming all those things l so desired to see in a partner.

One of the things l also had to change in my mindset was my approach to love. What the world is conveying as true and pure has quite a disillusion and damaging effect to what you would associate something as beautiful as love. We've been taught that no man is faithful no matter how holy he is, and to always leave room for disappointment when getting into relationships. That mantra has killed many dreams and relationships because it mentally prepares individuals for the worst. People pursue relationships even business in a fearful manner expecting that anything could go wrong at any given time. Many are living life on their toes. Why not leave room for success, peace, happiness and love? We ought to undo a lot of negative things engrafted in our minds. It does not matter what the world says, there is a truth that the One who authored love says.

In loving myself I also had to learn how to receive well without worrying that it may be too good to be true. For that to happen you have to be in a healthy place within yourself. Something that's unfamiliar to you cannot be received well. Society has programmed us to receive as little affection as possible because the rest is too corny. Based on the world standards, being too happy in a relationship signifies that there's something wrong. You can't be too happy, and if you're not fighting much, you're not being real with each other; so it is concluded that somebody is pretending. So much negativity has been associated with love.

This reminds me of an experience I had in a popular food outlet. Because of its location its normal to walk in, order and eat from a dirty table. One particular day when so starved, I walked in and ordered something to eat. But because of limited space, l had to sit at a dirty table. I was so unbothered by it because by now l was so used to it. One of the employees then came up to the table and started apologizing frantically and expressed how sorry she was that the table was dirty, whilst profusely cleaning it. I was stunned, this had never happened before. For someone to show so much concern that l was eating from a filthy place was somewhat new to me concerning its record of negligence. Over and over she apologized and l felt a sense of importance and being cared for. I liken this experience to love and relationships, one can get so accustomed to partaking from infidelity, lies and pain such that when peace, love and joy come; it is just so unfamiliar. When what's genuine finally settles in our hands, we become anxious and suspicious about it because we are so used to receiving the substandard. When you are so comfortable with being treated as unworthy, love can feel so foreign to you. Don't eat from a dirty table because it's something you have now adapted to; your standard should always be to eat from a clean one. If the place where you are neglects or does not live up to them, it is respectable to then shift to a different outlet. It should be so in love, don't settle for the heart shattering.

Women are taught to harden their hearts and build immunity against unpleasant things. Even if you see your partner being unfaithful turn a blind eye, he'll come around.

At times its concluded that you pushed him to do it, so you must work on yourself. You must change for your partner to be faithful to you, because it is you who is responsible for their indiscipline. It is said that infidelity is a hard pill to swallow but there's nothing you can do but accept it. They say our mothers, grandmothers and great grandmothers never found a solution to it but endured, so it's just the way of life and one should make peace with it. I refused to conform, I refused to believe that faithfulness was an illusion. Loving myself meant guarding my heart and peace. I wasn't going to be that woman keeping up appearances to get applause for sticking it through an extremely agonizing relationship yet I'm dying inside. The measure of women's strength is often determined by how much mistreatment they can endure. Their hearts have become so hardened that where one should naturally show emotion there is none; they've lost their ability to feel. Love is not pain, it is pure. When you leave a toxic relationship people will remark, where do you think you're going, it rains everywhere? We need a total remodel of our minds and how we look at love, relationships and marriage.

Love is not torment, neither does it make you lose your sanity. Do not conform to the worldly standards that, "it's not real till it hurts." You can be in love, but still be in sense. When it comes to love nobody can mistreat without your consent. When you are right within, those that come into your life won't have a choice but to measure up. Your best self, determines the character of people you allow into your life.

God is the author of love, to know Him is to know authentic love. There is no better way to learn authenticity than to turn to the one who created and authored it. What you desire does exist but when you are not right within yourself you become vulnerable to being preyed on. To get right within begins with getting right with God. He does the filling of love, peace, strength and grace in your heart. When you are filled to capacity it then becomes natural and undemanding to pour into other people because you are overflowing with goodness.

I had to do better not only for myself but for my daughter. She was going to learn from how I carry myself, so I needed to be a good example of what a woman of honor is. I needed to set the standard for her so that she too would never settle for less than God's very best. Faithfulness is not a myth. Obedience, discernment and walking in the will of God is what helps create authentic relationships. No man is perfect but a good one will have traits that make you see God in him. We often fall for the words instead of the fruits, we choose words over substance. Learn to love yourself, choose your heart.

Positive affirmation: Say out audibly; "I love myself."

PART 6

I LEARNED SELF-DISCIPLINE

———— ·•✦✦•· ————

Discipline is a life attribute that everyone should possess. It will account for the way you handle money, business, relationships, time and your emotions. A person without discipline is one without control of his or her essential being. They are soon influenced and swayed around by everything, even those that are unfavorable to their disposition and environment. Straying and negligence soon becomes an integral part of their character.

Be a person who is firm, objective and full of integrity so that you can handle life's responsibilities with so much power and moral uprightness. As an individual you have a part to play in things turning around for better in your life, and that is to learn discipline. Being disciplined is not only limited to sidestepping infidelity, it stretches to the way you spend money, time and above all, having disciplined thoughts. What thoughts are you allowing to dominate your mind?

Maturity also means being well-ordered. It's in the little things such as making time to read, exercise, pray, research or do things that build you. Some may have a shopping addiction, they always need to have the latest bag or shoe even if it may mean foregoing rent. For some it could be time management, they "turn up" but never seem to have the time to commit to something productive. For others it could be trying to give up smoking or excessive indulgence because of the health disadvantages. It could even be the simple discipline of learning to pick up a book, instead of your phone. We live in a world where dysfunction and immoral things are applauded. It is seen as normal and you are considered uninteresting if you are not living it up. This world needs you disciplined and mentally strong lest you be enticed by everything dangled in front of your eyes. Self-possession will preserve you, learn discipline.

Part of my growth in discipline entailed learning to manage my time better. It is factual that time cannot be recovered but rather redeemed. However, it does not mean it should not be accounted for. There is nothing as painful as looking back over your life with so much regret for the time you've wasted. Time is treasure and should be treated like a delicacy. Mostly when we don't know or understand our purpose we chase after everything or what is presented before us, reputably known as "go with the flow." It matters how you spend every minute, the relationships you choose to build, the opportunities you chase after and even time given to social media; be watchful of the time you apportion to it. All those are determining factors on how soundly you live your life.

I've learned to be a good steward over time. Since then I noticed how I began to have so much time in a day when I started giving attention to the right things; even my productivity increased. You can't live recklessly, you can't go anywhere and everywhere, you cannot just give your time to anybody because you are available. First thing you need to ask yourself is, "are they or is it worthy of my time?" Don't slack or slumber on time, use it wisely. Give your time to those well deserving and jealously guard it. You can't just pursue anything, is it worthy of your time? The way you use every second in a day should count for something well-meaning and when you've learned how to balance time, rest where needed because it is important that you take good care of body and mind. Maybe you feel a sense of regret over how you may have been careless with time. All hope is not lost, know that God can recycle time in the form of redemption, only He can make up for wasted years.

Discipline in finances is also crucial. There was a time in my life when everything I owned was fully paid for in cash. It may have not been worth millions but I owned it and owed no one nothing but love. I bought my first television set without a basic salary, after having taken care of my rent and other responsibilities I would still have enough left over. Not a big deal you may think, but you must appreciate the fact that, for somebody who was a waitress surviving on tips and commission at the time; this was such a huge accomplishment for me. Technically speaking 1 may have just been wealthier than some. It so happened that in that period 1 wanted a very expensive pair of jeans from a popular retailer, but its cost was almost equivalent to a month's rent. As somebody without a basic salary this was a serious dismay to me, how was 1 ever going to be able to afford them? Being the resolute person 1 was, 1 committed to saving up. I had to forgo a few things but ultimately 1 was able to afford those jeans because 1 had the discipline of saving money.

Overtime my life changed and 1 progressed, but 1 soon noticed how the more 1 earned, the more 1 became irresponsible with money. I would open clothing accounts and buy anything without preplanning. If 1 wanted something and didn't have the money, 1 would simply create debt and pay for it later on. It always starts off with small amounts that you think you can write off then it escalates to ones you struggle to pay off. The discipline you have in little is the discipline you should have in abundance.

Take a moment to self-introspect on where you need to apply a little more discipline in your life. Are you disciplined?

---••❦••---

Refuse to go through an encounter and remain the
same. Never let any experience go to waste, let it
teach you something, let it
make you better. And when you have learned, let it
pour hope into somebody else. Your scars are a
testament to what you've survived,
let it empower another. Fulfillment is when your story
has changed another.

---••❦••---

I LEARNED FROM MY LESSONS

--------- ••✧✦✧•• ---------

If there is one thing you should never allow, is falling so hard and getting back up the same. Each experience teaches you something but often we find ourselves going around in circles because we refuse to learn a particular lesson. When you fall, let it not just be dust or bruises you pick up from the ground. Rise up with a lesson and wisdom. Rise up with a new stride and strength to kick from your path what tripped you the first time. Rise up with better vision and focus, your mandate being to conquer. Rise up with better perspective and determination, rise up with a solid walk.

You weren't designed to go through the same thing over and over again without any real change, it is unreasonable to be going through the same cycle of things every year. Learn the lesson now and move on, refuse to be stuck in one area. Maturity is acknowledging that you made a mistake, take responsibility for it, grow and learn to do better. You got away with it the first time, second and the third, do not wait for things to take a turn for the worst before you finally get the point. And when you've learned, share that wisdom with the world, somebody really needs it.

The things that aided you, made you whole are not meant to be kept a secret, they are intended to be shared so somebody can be saved from *I Learned My Lessons* moments of "l wish l knew then what l know now." I purposed that as long as there is life in me, l would share my wisdom with the world and no woman would go through what l did if it can be avoided. You are on the right path when you don't want the bad things that happened to you, happening to somebody else. Your story is meant to change, and give wisdom and knowledge to another.

As l grew l began to make better choices. Every decision is substantial, no matter how insignificant you may perceive it to be. Always take a moment to sit down and think things through, not over dinner, stuck in traffic, at the gym or lunch hour at work. Find a quiet place to sit, away from all the clatter and take time to think long and hard on every choice you plan on making. Thinking in snippets and impulsively has never brought about wise decisions. In the past I've gotten into misfortune for the simple fact that l just didn't take time to think. Some of the things l experienced were necessary, some were not. Be careful that you are not in agony because of bad decisions, it is very easy to mistake adversity for righteousness rather than what it truly is, "that is sin."

You can find that you are rooted in one place because you refuse to learn, and until that lesson is learned; you can never reach the next level of elevation. Sometimes stagnation is a result of repeated choices and decisions. Until your choices change, your life remains the same. As you mature gain that ability to make better choices.

In my personal experiences everything served its purpose and part of it was learning what l did not know, and when l did; l vowed to do better. I refused to keep doing the same things over and over but somehow miraculously expecting different and better results.

The choices we make have a way of descending through our bloodline, the cut off is where we start making better choices. Imagine a generation of men and women who fear God and wouldn't compromise obedience for anything. When you know better, you do better; you're that powerful that you can impact a whole generation.

Your decisions can affect a whole lineage, so, before you make that decision, think of how it's going to affect the generations coming after you. Whatever you act on comes with consequences of either good or bad.

Learn from your lessons and make better choices.

Positive affirmation: Say out audibly; "l make sound decisions."

Out of your current disadvantage, there's a hidden advantage. Dry seasons are refining seasons. Your character is being shaped and inner being made resilient. You are being pruned for prominence.

DRY SEASONS REFINED ME

————··◆✿◆··————

Dry seasons are there to birth something in you and build inner strength and resilience. Those seasons refine character and birth boldness, kindness, prayer, discipline, confidence, patience, humility, forgiveness, loyalty, truth and honesty.

This season necessitates trimming, grooming and the pruning process to remove the worst and instill the best in you. The same way a tree is pruned is the same way you are refined. Dry seasons are where God is saying, "let's remove that anger, bitterness and unforgiveness. Let's get rid of that low self-esteem and remove that hurt you've carried for so long. Let's fix that poor decision making and complacency mindset, lets deal with the root of that issue. Let's rid you of pride and selfishness. You won't be able to handle marriage, money or do business with that kind of attitude. You can't be a wealthy person who is unwilling to give or a leader who is rude and prideful. For where you're headed you can't take that with you, let's get you wise and prayed up." Some things God will hold off not because he doesn't want you to have them, but for the reason that He needs you to become the person who has the character and responsibility to handle it. I became grateful for the things that God did not release into my life till 1 grew, matured and became gentle, patient and kinder.

As you go through dry seasons it feels like death but when you see the results of what is birthed out of pain, it soon makes you forget the anguish you went through. Watch the wholesome person you'll become, the books you will write, the businesses, the people you'll help and the peace that will flood your mind. The wisdom in it all supersedes the pain. John 16:21 mentions that:

> *"When a woman gives birth, she has a hard time, there's no getting around it. But when the baby is born, there is joy in the birth. This new life in the world wipes out memory of the pain." (NKJV)*

I am so grateful for my dry season because of all the unhealthy things that God removed in me and the amazing he replaced it with. I needed to be in my fullness first and needed to be pruned for prominence. I was coming up short in some areas and this is the season that God used to refine me. I was purified in the furnace of affliction and refined in adversity. I learned humility and matured, I became wiser and patient. I learned how to give more, to be kinder and extend grace to others. My heart became so tender and 1 was often heartened to pray for other people, even some I had never met. I found myself praying for other people even in moments when 1 needed it more. I learned to be selfless and more giving. On the outside it looked as if 1 was wasting away, but on the inside true character was being molded.

In general, when you become an overall better person, certain things just begin to flourish. As l began to get my priorities right, l became more responsible. I found myself striving to be a better mother and individual.

I had to step up for my daughter so she could have a positive role model to look up to. I realized that my ministry was first to my child and l but for a long time, it had been about finding the "one" then becoming a happy family.

Dry seasons brought me to a moment of saying, "God thank you that it fell apart. Thank you for the rejection, thank you for the betrayal, thank you that l didn't get that job. Thank you for those who didn't answer their phones when l needed help, it taught me how to truly depend on You for everything; it taught me to seek You first." In the moment it was happening it felt like torture but it pushed me to greater. I never knew l could be an author and dream bigger, all this shaped my character. It taught me forgiveness and to be compassionate and more giving. The lessons that came from it all were valuable and out of my greatest pain, is the most I've ever grown in all the years that I've been on this earth. As God began to strip me of everything that wasn't like Him it felt as if l was becoming somebody brand new.

In my dry seasons is where the fruits of the Spirit were birthed and fully developed in me. Peace, patience, kindness and love. I learned how to be empathetic and became more understanding of people's situations. I took note of the times l wasn't as giving as l should have been. There were things l could have forgone to help somebody who really needed it and even pay my tithe. There is a lot of controversy surrounding tithe and l sought to truly understand it for myself. One of the things that came to light was that the same way praying doesn't help God, is the same way giving doesn't. How do you give to someone who created and owns everything? It's about the principle, it keeps your heart grounded and ensures you are always connected to the source. Giving refines your character and stirs your capacity to be a charitable person. If you can give to somebody who owns everything, you can give to your neighbor or a person in need. Do for others what you wish would have been done for you, in your moments of desperation and need.

What dry season are you in? Let the process birth and nurture character in you. There is a hidden advantage, in your current disadvantage.

———•♦✧❧♦•———

In your journey let those who walk into your life find you complete and serene. When you're self-sufficient emotionally, you become shatterproof. Should you encounter those with ulterior motives, they will shake you but not break you. Strive to be whole, strive to be a beautiful spirit.

———•♦✧❧♦•———

PART 7

I DEALT WITH THE ROOT OF MY ISSUES

————————·•✦·——————————

S ome time ago I joined a challenge on Facebook hosted by a Christian couple that strives to build more godly marriages. This is were they invite all singles to pray for their future spouses for five consecutive days, and also have live webinars and invite guest speakers to share words of wisdom.

On one particular webinar one of the ladies spoke about "dealing with the root of your issues" because, so many people get into dysfunctional relationships founded on underlying things they haven't confronted. Others began to acknowledge what they carried; rage, bitterness and unforgiveness because of the things they had experienced in the past and currently.

I sat there reflecting and trying to figure out what mine could possibly be and it dawned on me that, for the longest time I struggled with self-esteem issues. It emanated from the fact that I had a child soon after high school and somebody said to me; "now that you have child, who is going to want to marry you?" This wasn't said out of scorn, but rather sympathy and concern. You must understand that I came from a society that cringed upon a man marrying a woman with a child or children. Some would even consider it such a disgrace. Some people would say to me, l will struggle to get a husband so its best l narrow down my choices to divorcees and men with children. I couldn't understand why they saw me and those they referenced that way; "as not good enough." For many years l carried that with me and saw myself as damaged goods, so each time a man approached me, l would take it as a compliment. In my mind they were doing me a favor by even considering to be with me. I would secretly say, "at least they are asking me out on dates." l longed for acceptance and to hear someone say that l was enough, even if l had a child. It was that feeling that at least somebody is looking in my direction, so l should be grateful lest it slips through my fingers. l did not even realize what a toxic mindset I carried. In some moments when people would ask why I'm still not married, my response would be, "maybe its because l have a child." I had the unhealthiest self-image, I was looking for approval and validation.

I would date people who would physically and mentally abuse me and blame myself for it. Maybe if l never talked back or questioned their inconsistencies and infidelity they would have treated me better. What l did not realize was that l was the favor, l was the prize and deserved to be treated like royalty. But let me tell you the moment l got a revelation of who l was, l began to carry myself differently. I became confident, strong and valued myself; 1 truly began to love myself. You determine the atmosphere within and around you, let your aura be that of calm and gentleness. The world is only as better as your inner disposition, and what you choose to add to it.

I dealt with that root issue of self-esteem, 1 stopped seeing myself as an indigent but instead honorable. I stopped downplaying my value for men who were not worthy of the woman 1 was. The way 1 perceived and received love was elevated.

To never give up and win you have to confront those underlying issues. It could be anger from childhood traumas, bitterness from past heartbreaks or unforgiveness. Some are seeking for comfort from their brokenness, some came from broken families and didn't have a good example of love so, they walk right into dysfunction. Some lacked proper mentoring and guidance, others are looking for father figures in their partners, some for healing and wholeness. Others are so deeply scarred such that they see the world as a place of torment, and no longer care to subject themselves to abuse or anything negative that hinders them from becoming the imminent version of themselves.

For how long will you allow it to hold you back? Deal with it!

I DEVELOPED A HEALTHY SELF IMAGE

---·•❧•·---

Most nights before 1 go to bed, 1 usually take a moment to listen to worship music because of the peace and serenity it brings. One particular evening, 1 got so lost in the power of the song and midway through it, God whispered to my heart; "if you knew who you are, you would carry yourself differently, yes you are amazing, you just don't know it yet."

I immediately broke down in tears of gratitude. This meant so much for my heart given that 1 was healing from demeaning words that had been spoken to me. In that moment God reminded me of the phenomenal woman 1 am.

In life we go through so much heartache, pain and rejection such that we soon forget who we are and walk around with drooping heads. It doesn't matter who belittled you, wrote you off, made you feel worthless or implied that you are inferior and don't measure up. The truth is you are royalty, even in times when it is not acknowledged or validated by man. When God has put His stamp of approval on you, nobody should make you feel any less or have leeway to approach you with insufficiencies.

After that night I woke up with so much confidence and high esteem and that's the internal stature God desires for every single woman to possess because, it is what will determine the character of people you will allow into your life. From that moment on, never again did 1 struggle with self-esteem issues, God dealt with it in depth, from the inside out. I saw myself the way He saw me, a woman of grace, strength and ability, a rare gem.

I began to see myself as the woman who could be the first of something in her family, a woman unlimited. A woman who can walk into a boardroom and close a business deal. A woman who can empower others because of what she has survived. A woman who understands that her dreams are not unattainable but can be achieved. A woman of greatness and skills, and finds fulfillment in showing kindness to those in need. A good mother and homemaker who keeps it peaceful. I became that woman who can make better choices, and so 1 walked in the boldness of who 1 am.

Yes!!!!! That's exactly how God had seen me all along and 1 had finally tapped into that revelation.

Until a woman is at her best self, she will constantly entertain the same character of men. It is important for every woman to have a healthy self-image because often where worth is not known, anything goes. Walk in the truth of that you are worth so much more. A better relationship begins with a healthy self-image. A woman with high self-esteem makes better relationship choices because she has a revelation of who she really is. Hold yourself in high regard and you will never settle for anything less than you comprehend you deserve.

When somebody does not reciprocate your kindness or love let it not take away from who you are. Just because they do not see or discern what you carry, does not mean your value is invalid or non-existent. Jesus was not welcome in a lot of places but it did not change that he was the son of God.

When 1 look at some of the people 1 entertained in the past, it made me realize that there was a flaw in me that needed to be addressed. What was that thing that made me look at something and say it was good, yet factually it was toxic? It was lack of wisdom and fear that if 1 missed this chance 1 might never get another. Little did 1 know how valuable, special and set apart 1 was and that the man 1 would finally settle with, will be beyond blessed.

The people that may have hurt you in the past were wrong in every sense. Nothing can ever justify what they did, but recognize that your accountability was in you allowing it to happen. So, lets fix you, lets elevate your confidence so that anybody who doesn't come right, can never have access to your heart. Let's get you wiser and more discerning. When

you are where you're supposed to be internally, you begin to
repel certain things.

As a well-known quote says,
"you date at the level of your self-esteem," begin to see
yourself as a gift to this world because you are and so
much more.

---·◆❦◆·---

Ageless beauty is that of true inner self. Adorn the right one, let the outward appearance be validation of what is within. The beauty in your spirit does not fade away but outward appearance gradually wanes. When concealer and lipstick can no longer cover much, let the world see the sensual woman with poise that you are because what sustains you, is on the inside of you. Until outer beauty com-
            plements the inner, it is vain......

---·◆❦◆·---

I WORKED ON MY INNER BEAUTY

As a woman I find myself in moments where I spend so much time in front of the mirror, enhancing my features. Not that there is anything wrong with taking care of yourself but one of the most important things I've come to understand is; what is on the outside should complement what is on the inside, and not cover what is non-existent. 1st peter 3 vs 2-5 restates:

> *"Don't be concerned about the outward beauty of fancy hairstyles, expensive jewelry, or beautiful clothes. You should clothe yourself instead with the beauty that comes from within, the unfading beauty of a gentle and quiet spirit, which is so precious to God."*
> *(NLT)*

Concealer can only hide so much, it is soon wiped off and at day end, you have to look in the mirror and be at peace with the woman you are. There is no amount of makeup or clothes that you can adorn yourself with that will make you truly alluring than what you carry on the inside of you.

It is now that I fully appreciate that true beauty and luminance come from the God within you. Zechariah 2:5 cast light upon my eyes and heart on that truth.

> *"And I'll be right there with her, a radiant presence within."*
> *(MSGE)*

In the world we live in many get into debt because of clothing accounts, they are so focused on the outside for the cause that, it is what validates them to themselves and other people. I used to be of the mind that validation is always from other people, until l got the revelation that self-acceptance is also a struggle for some. They don't feel adequate if they are not best dressed or wearing make-up, and because they are not accepting of themselves, being validated by ornaments and others is consoling.

All those things that make you pleasing to the eye are good but their purpose shouldn't be to conceal an unhealthy self-image or what is missing within you. It will make you attractive for those few moments but what happens behind closed doors? We often long for others to gaze into our eyes and appraise us with words of endearment; "I love you, l appreciate you, you are beautiful." And when it never comes, we feel a sense of emptiness and that we don't measure up. When will you take a moment to deeply look into your eyes through the mirror and affirm to yourself what you so desire to hear from other people? Even if you don't say it out loud that inner belief of the noteworthy woman you are should be strongly present such that when you come around other people, you don't feel inferior. Never become so self-concerned that you neglect grooming your inner being.

Inner beauty begins with knowing Christ, when He is the source of your confidence and charm, then what's on the outside is simply counterbalancing what is rooted within. When God bared it all before me of the woman l am, it seized to be about dressing and cosmetics. Knowing who l carried within, made me feel my greatest more than any wardrobe change could ever achieve. Until you do the internal work needed, you will always look for outside factors to make you feel you are enough. A time came when God had truly secured me on the inside that l began to care less whether I was wearing the latest designer shoe. I still took great care of myself but wasn't unsettled with the price tag on my clothes because on the inside; l was full. I was enough and that's the way it should it be.

Work on your inner disposition.

Rejection is sometimes a set up for you to collide with purpose. In the moment it doesn't seem anything like it, but rest in knowing that anything that led you to your destiny is not a waste. Those who misused or never cherished your value, only means they did not have a revelation of who you are.

I LET GO

———— •◦🜂◦• ————

If I held on to the past or refused to let certain things go, I wouldn't be where I am today. I cannot fathom the amazing people and opportunities I would have been deprived of. I would have missed out on writing a book that will change the world, and also forfeited purpose. Each time I think of how I almost lost out on destiny because of a few bad choices, I go down on my knees and thank God for loving me the way He does. God is not the "Yes man," He will say NO at times for your preservation and well-being. If He withheld it from you it means it was never good as quoted in Psalms 84:11:

> *"No good thing will he withhold from those who*
> *walk uprightly."*
> *(NKJV)*

Take that risk and release everything that's been holding you back.

Sometimes it will take making a conscious decision to say, "I will forget everything that happened. Yes, it was unfair, it was unimaginable pain and I thought I was going to lose my mind. But if I could just forget and dare and to press on and believe that as groundless as it may seem, I can recover and take my power back. Yes, the process will be tumultuous and I'll get frustrated sometimes but if I can endure, what's on the other side is far greater than my yesterday; "the opposite of loss is gain." Begin to take thinking as something that can be a deliberate thing, what can be termed "on purpose thinking." And when you commit to developing a positive mindset, you are taking your life back.

The best way to deal with rejection and a toxic past is to let go of the ones who caused it. Letting go often feels as if you are releasing something you'll never be able to replace, but what you may not realize is; when they left you, they left favor, they left power and the presence of greatness. There are people who are going to miss out on certain things because they chose not to stick it out with you. They lost, you didn't.

I made a conscience decision to release my past from my hands. I called my mind to attention, acknowledged and accepted what was happening at that particular period then one emotion at a time, I began to let go. There is nothing I desired from what I had left behind, instead I wanted better for me. For the first time I truly believed that I too deserved the best of everything and that it wasn't just for a select few.

I also let go of wrath, bitterness and frustration for my well-being and liberation. See it this way, God could have let you have it but it was going to burn you. He sees the end from the beginning, He sees what you cannot with the naked eye. He knew how distressful life would have been had you chosen that path. You thought you had it right but what you did not realize is that you would have chosen a lifetime of grief. So, let it go and trust God for better. At times a door closed by men is not one that was opened by God to begin with, find peace in knowing that if it's from Him, it shall surely open. Maybe your situation does not involve an individual, but damaging emotions that you need to release. What are those things you need to lose a grip of? Is it anger, unforgiveness, pain or bitterness. Release it from your heart into the hands of God.

Letting go will also mean releasing people who are disloyal to you. Disloyalty is not only limited to relationships, but can apply in business and other areas of life. I used to be a person who worried so much about what people thought of me. I desperately wanted to be in everyone's good books. It mattered to me how they felt about me and 1 was uneasy if they weren't saying the right things in my absence. I would always be quick to defend myself in their eyes if there was ever any negative news about me. Its not a terrible thing to rise to your defense but the only thing wrong with that picture is that, it goes against everything loyalty is. You can't control what people say in your absence, you can't control loyalty. If you've truly shown your sincerity to people and it just never seems enough, release them peacefully. Know that if your experiences led you to God and to your destiny, it is not a loss.

Let it go…..

I GAINED WISDOM AND DISCERN-MENT

---·•◦⟨⟩◦•·---

WISDOM

To be wise in mind and not in action is knowledge gone to waste. There were moments in my life l knew the right thing to do but just didn't do it. But as l grew and learned, l gained wisdom. I became a person with good judgement and it soon became evident that, growth is applied knowledge. It showed in my composure, choices and discipline and brought me to a place of so much reverence for God for the wisdom He poured into me. After a thread of terrible choices l pleaded with Him for wisdom, I desired to do better and develop into a woman who was upright. Maybe you too need wisdom, God is ever ready to freely give it, as pointed out in James 1:5:

> *"If you need wisdom, ask our generous God, and He will give it to you."(NLT)*

Growing in wisdom will also mean chasing after knowledge and learning new things. Don't be ashamed if you are not naturally born with an ability. I strongly believe that you can learn, perfect and master a skill. There are things I've had to learn with the understanding that knowledge carries a lot of virtue, and with it comes liberation. There is also an invaluable discovery l made as l amassed wisdom. Many a time when you have not overcome a situation, there is a possibility that there is a particular truth you have not uncovered about it. John 8:32 reads:

"And you will know the truth, and the truth will set you free."
(NLT)

What circumstance are you faced with today? There is a "knowing" that needs to happen, so that you can break free from what's been holding you down. How much do you know?

DISCERNMENT

When 1 gained discernment, 1 became cautious of the people 1 allow into my life. We keep people in our lives completely blind to the fact that they are the reason certain things haven't gotten to us. Watch who you build with, especially who you decide to marry. Think for a moment; how many years are you behind because of that one person you chose to hold onto? Who and where could you have been had it not been for them? How much time have you wasted holding onto the wrong person or thing? The emphasis being on people because many struggle with establishing genuine relationships; especially romantic ones.

1st Samuel 16:7 says:
"Men and women look at the face; God looks into the heart."

(MSGE)

Discernment taught me to look at the inner actuality of a person. Grow in your ability to judge well, it will save your heart. What misinformed judgements have you made in the past that need to be adjusted?

As you become more discerning, I can't ignore the fact that you cannot lone exist. As large as the aero plane is, it has a weakness that it cannot reverse. In an airport procedure called, "pushback" the aircraft is pushed by a mule to face the direction from which it wishes to take off. If you could see how much smaller the mule is, you could never imagine that it can have the capacity to push a plane.

This goes to show that no matter how great and matured you've become, you will need people around you, to move in on the things you don't have the capability of. You cannot do life solely by yourself, therefore it is important that you create legitimate relationships and friendships. At some point you will need somebody, but make sure that you are getting help from people of integrity and respect. The reality is nobody can do everything. A pilot doesn't automatically have the knowledge to sail a ship, neither does he instantly become a chef or possess the skills to coach a football team. People working together balance each other out, you can be the best at what you do, and others the best at what they do.

Association will require communication, be watchful of what you say and whom you say it to in the event that you need to vent. It is not a bad thing to seek wise counsel but I truly believe that if you spend time in the presence of God and enquire of Him, He will begin to show you hidden solutions. I know you want to be heard but let God be your biggest confidant, vent to Him first before anyone lest He give you a solution on an issue that no one else should have been privy to. Guarding your heart also means bridling your tongue.

This also applies to those who do you wrong. Learn to say as little as possible, it's not every emotion that should be expressed verbally. Often when we are wronged we feel the need to rise to our defense, so we kick, scream and shout because we want to be heard. But I have since learned that a reaction can sometimes make you look imprudent, gain mastery over your emotions. At times the things we wrestle are not physical.

Ephesians 6:12 in its opening line reads: "We are not fighting against human beings, but against the spiritual wicked forces."
(GNT)

The more you say the worse you escalate things. Don't get the last word, at the expense of looking foolish. Others may seem to be having their moment let them be. Do what will edify you, whether it's in releasing your emotions, or an argument with somebody; say as little as possible. Address each episode at its level, for some issues you will have to fight on your knees, in others; a spoken word will do. Be discerning of which to apply.

For your daily walk you will need wisdom and discernment, call for them and the One who gives without limits, will pour into you.

Don't think of money as something to be made and
withheld. Being wealthy comes with the
responsibility of showing kindness to those
in need. Let your desire for financial freedom
encompass the many who will
benefit from it.

I CHANGED MY MENTAL WEALTH

There was a time 1 never quite understood what people meant by, "poverty mentality." Its not that 1 did not have the rational capacity to catch on, but 1 wanted to understand it in layman's terms. I knew 1 wanted to be wealthy so definitely that wasn't a poverty mindset, right? What I didn't realize is you can know something, but not see anything at all. I desired to be wealthy but didn't quite have a mental picture of what it meant to be financially free at that particular level. I soon grasped the intended meaning that many want to be wealthy, but few can see beyond where they currently are.

A poverty mentality is the inability to see yourself moving beyond who you are and where you currently are. It is limitation in your visualization. Certain people are where they are because that's as far as they can see, where they are is all they know. If you are comfortable with where you are, you won't desire change. It's a mentality because you have to picture something first. Changing environments can help you build but if your mental wealth doesn't change, you can be deprived in the wealthiest land.

Most millionaires didn't get there by mistake, it was already blueprinted in their minds. They elevated their minds to that level of wealth. Some are fortunate to be born into an empire, but for the majority it is things they worked for and built; and it all started with raising their mental wealth. In their minds they saw multi-million-dollar ideas, estates, and businesses. With that said I've learned that one should also give time to wealth generation because it is not always instant, it may take a while. With every level of success you attain, know that you never stop growing.

To break out of something you have to see beyond it. Mentally prepare yourself for wealth. Personally, I knew that being an author and aspiring entrepreneur comes with challenges but if l was prepared in my mind, l would push through with courage. Somebody once said, "being an employee is hard and so is being an entrepreneur, you just have to choose your hard." In the past l had tried to be an employee, l got so many great opportunities but they were always momentary, there was never a time that l was offered a permanent position. In all my years as an employee l had never received a bonus, I would sweat and fully pledge to my work but was never rewarded for it. If l wanted more money l would have to work overtime. When others were making plans for their bonuses, the new cars and assets they would acquire, l was trying to figure out how best l could make ends meet.

In one particular company l didn't even qualify for a simple uniform because it was only for permanent employees. After having worked for that company for about four years, my contract was terminated unexpectedly. I was sent my way with no gratuity or compensation to show that I had worked for that organization for that period of a time. There are people across borders who have been on contracts for ten years, even more without benefits.

In my life I did want to be an employee but it just didn't seem to be working for me. My prayers soon changed from "Lord I need a job, to Lord I need business ideas." Working for other people seemed to have failed so I went on a quest to discover a different avenue of generating money. Two scenarios I looked at was the idea of picking up a new set of skills, instead of a second job because the former is a long-term investment towards permanent financial freedom. That is the mindset I started grooming and that majority should also possess. When you refuse to raise your mental wealth, you rob yourself of financial freedom.

In your quest for wealth don't disregard the place of God in it. Deuteronomy 8:18 says:

> "Remember the Lord your God. He is the one who gives you power to be successful." (NLT)

Business ideas, skills and ability come from God. When His hand is on your works, achievement is guaranteed. Do you need to re-evaluate and raise your mental wealth? Begin to challenge yourself to see greater in your mind. Your pocket is as large as the capacity of your mind.

---◆❦◆---

There is no soldier who has ever gone to war without training.

Sometimes what looks like punishment, is preparation for your next level. It builds tenacity and patience to withstand the boisterous winds that may threaten to derail you off your path. Your latter needs you stronger, wiser, matured and more courageous. After endurance, comes the promise.

You are not being punished, you are becoming.

---◆❦◆---

I ENDURED

The things you go through are a molding process of what you are becoming. Endurance is a series of coming to something. Some seasons are there to build and bring forth the light hidden within you. The place where you are headed will need you more courageous, full of faith, wisdom and discernment, it will need you bolder and confident. In the moment you don't understand because you haven't seen what the latter looks like but when you finally get to see it, it will make sense why you had to endure so much. You'll understand why you had to be betrayed that way and why you had to be broken beyond reason.

In that uncomfortable moment of enduring learn to say to yourself, "it hurts but I'm becoming, l may not understand but I'm becoming." If you can endure, what's on the other side is much more glorious. When you finally get to hold the promise in your hands, it will make sense why certain things had to happen the way they did. There is peace, liberty, greatness, breakthroughs and mending that follow after you have endured. Because you never gave up, but held on and believed things could get better; it soon becomes so. The triumph will be worth the endurance. There shall be restoration of everything material or immaterial, I make to reference to 1st Peter 5:10:

"And after you have suffered a little while, the God of all of grace, who called you to His eternal glory in Christ will Himself restore, confirm, strengthen and establish you." (ESV)

In training, strength comes from those things you never imagined you could survive, or what you thought would completely wipe you out. The things I suffered matured me fully. Endurance builds strength and character so I endured, I held on to my positive confessions and never gave up.

Endurance will make you stronger, you will get to a place where you begin to see yourself surviving impossible situations and that's when you know that you are ready for your elevation. Your mental grit has been built and you have developed strength of mind. What you patiently endure, becomes tomorrow's strength. For your next level you can't afford to be lacking in strength and resilience. If you can endure what's on the other side is much more beautiful.

When you have fully matured, the negative things that may happen in your next level won't move you because, you have developed the mental capacity to handle it. The same way you can't fit into a shoe you wore when you were ten years old; is similar to that the things which scarred you years ago, won't have the same effect. You outgrow certain things, you handle them better. You brush off gossip, instead of the way you would want to confront every single person who spoke ill of you. You see rejection as opportunity to grow into your calling.

When 1 though 1 was being broken, 1 was actually being positioned for purpose. My season of endurance taught me to be still and recognize that the Lord He is God. I never quite understood that, till 1 came to a place where 1 felt 1 had exhausted every option 1 though possible; but still didn't have a solution. But there is a place of rest in God that comes after you have outwardly chased everything you thought would work. You finally leave it in His hands and hear Him say; "I know you don't understand, but 1 got this." Then peace, you're no longer anxious. As you endure, be still means you're not in this alone, it means you don't have to figure out everything on your own. It means whichever way things go, God is in control. It wouldn't make sense for God to give you purpose but say the rest you'll figure out on your own.

The hardest part is holding on through the confusion. When you don't fully understand why things are happening the way they are, you will think it's the end, but God can see that you'll survive. In my own battles and season of endurance the enemy tried to pull me back into hopelessness but I had to fight back and declare "Lord you are God." I developed a certain level of resistance to bad thoughts that tried to weigh me down. I know your problems may seem undefeatable but some day they will be your victory song. Have you held on long enough? Don't let go until you're holding victory in your hands. The ending you hope for will come.

Hold on......

I FOUND PEACE IN GOD THROUGH MEDITATION

———··◆✦◆··———

When you meditate you are focusing your mind on something for a period of time, but it matters what it is that you are thinking on. When going through adversity individuals tend to give too much attention to everything unpleasant that may be happening in their lives. That is why it is of the greatest importance that you train your mind to make that quick shift of moving from negative thoughts, to ones that are constructive.

Your mind is something that can be trained and mastered so that you are in better control of your thoughts. There is something that I've learned to do overtime when I find my mind lingering and moving in the direction of negativity. I quickly call my mind to attention meaning, I immediately shut down negative thoughts in that very moment and begin to focus my mind on what the word of God says about my situation. It could be being healed, becoming whole, excelling and whatever good thing I may need. Why the word of God? Because that is where His promises are hidden. Promises of peace, good success, love, marriage, wealth and all things beautiful.

Meditation shifts your focus onto the truth of the word of God from your current circumstance. It allows the truth of His word to permeate your mind and heart. Meditation helps you hide the word of God in your heart so that in times of trouble, you are pulling strength from within. When you've done so, you understand that no matter what may be happening around you; there's a greater power on the inside of you.

With meditation also comes peace. The word of God is comforting, so when you think on it, you're often accompanied with an overwhelming sense of peace that everything is going to be alright. It makes you focus on the certainty of the word of God. What is the last thing you think on before you go to bed? Is it that last video clip you saw on your social media newsfeed, a song you listened to, the movie you watched on television or something you read on the internet. Whatever it is was it positive? What is your mind active with when you go to bed? What is the first thing you wake up to each morning? Funny social media statuses, a word of inspiration or a moment of prayer? What sets the tone of your day? Be careful of what you allow to lodge in your mind, be it from social media, people or whatever platform, always ensure that its things that build. What you feed your mind, turns into a principle and belief in your heart.

I came to a place in my life where for every trial I found counsel and peace in God. Whenever I felt overwhelmed, God became my safe haven. This is where I began to derive everything; peace, joy, happiness, strength, confidence, reassurance, closure and understanding. For everything 1 lacked He became my supreme and ultimate source, 1 stopped searching in other places. When 1 was wounded, broken, bleeding, feeling defeated, my war cry became "Jesus."

The things around you shouldn't determine your peace and joy because the day they don't deliver; you will be the crankiest person. When God is your peace things may not be working around you but still, when you read His word, His Spirit becomes so strong in you and gives you authority and grace to face life with strength and courage. There is a kind of peace that is only found in God. Where you can be in the middle of the harshest storm, but still be at harmony. That peace is found in the word of God. As you meditate you are echoing the promises of God over and over in your mind. It somehow helps clear the clutter and brings you to a place of stillness and calm.

"What are you meditating on? Isaiah 26:3 says:
"You keep him in perfect peace whose mind is stayed on you, because he trusts in you." (ESV)

Focus your mind on the word of God, so that peace can flood your life.

CONCLUSION

DON'T GIVE UP!

————··✦❀✦··————

A couple of years ago just before 1 turned twenty-two, 1 had an opportunity to work for an insurance company. It was a fair job with a decent salary and good working conditions. I had a lovely office which 1 shared with a colleague but right across the street was one of the most reputable banks in town. Day after day 1 would just gaze at the building with its iconic key logo at the top and just imagine myself working there. I would picture myself strutting my heels through the office in my neatly pressed uniform.

I would day dream about rubbing shoulders with the elite and my career just shooting out the roof. I did not know how or when it would happen, all 1 knew was that 1 wanted to work for one of the most prestigious banks in the country. But there was one problem; "1 was unqualified." I barely had a diploma, hadn't attended university because when everybody else went off to start their semesters, 1 was raising a baby. At the time 1 didn't have much of a prayer life and barely understood the foundational concept of taking things to the Lord in prayer, but 1 knew 1 needed a miracle. Despite my qualification predicament my eyes were so fixated on making it into the banking sector; that's all could think of. One day l gathered the courage to take my chances and drop off my resume at their offices. Nobody told me they were hiring neither had there been any post advertised but none the less, l went ahead because, once a dreamer starts; there's no stopping them.

As l waited in anticipation for a favorable response there is a famous quote l stood by quite a lot that says, "what the mind perceives and believes; that it can achieve." Because my understanding was so limited, I did not know that l was empowering my mind with that kind of positive thinking. As impossible as the circumstances looked, l began to picture that dream becoming a reality. A few weeks down the line when l least expected, l received a call for an interview invite. I could not believe it!!

This newly single mother was finally getting a shot at an opportunity she had dreamed of for so long. Days before the interview l prepared myself mentally, and made sure l did all l could to leave the best impression possible. On arrival for my interview l felt a bit intimidated because l was up against people with college degrees and had so much more work experience than l did, but l still gave it my best shot. After the interview they were to inform us telephonically or post the results. When l finally got my response, it wasn't the best of news, they had given the job to somebody else. l was devastated.

For some reason l did not let that deter me, one day during my lunch hour l walked into that bank and asked to see the manager who had interviewed us. Fortunately, he agreed to see me and l explained to him why l was there. I told him that l needed help with pin pointing where l went wrong in my interview so l could do better next time. In my hand l had a pen and notepad and wrote down what he shared, and the mistakes l had made. He was surprised to say the least and applauded my bravery and resilience. l sincerely thanked him for his time and l was off. After that l felt a sense of peace.

Life went on, then two weeks later l received an unexpected call from the bank, and l could not process what l was just about to hear. They were calling to let me know that there was an opening at one of their other branches and l came highly recommended by one of the managers. There was no need to be re-interviewed and l was to start work in a few days. As soon as l hung up the phone l fell on my knees and shouted, "thank you Jesus" and tears just began to stream down my face. I could not believe that such a wonderful thing was happening to somebody like me. And so, the countdown to my new job began, I had my medical examination done that was paid for by the company. All that was left, was for me to show up at the office. When l started working there it was everything l thought it would it be, just the way l had imagined it.

Why am I sharing this story? After all these years it made me realize that sometimes we are just a thought away from completely altering our lives. I assure you; if you can see it with the eye of your mind first, you can have it. When you begin to see the impossible being a reality, it will change your life. Whether it's healing, business, marriage and success, whatever that is pure and true that you desire; it can be yours. What I couldn't quite understand at the time is that, that's exactly how faith works. It's when you see things that haven't manifested yet, becoming a reality. So, from this moment on, stretch your mind, empower it and begin to see things that you've desired for so long, coming true. Begin to see your situation getting better, your life coming together and things falling into place.

Positive thinking did a lot for my faith and personal growth. My perspective changed on a lot of things, and I somehow began to see a way out of anything.

With God all things are possible, align your mind to His word and watch the miraculous happen in your life.

DON'T GIVE UP!